Writing Workouts That Work

A Coach's Playbook
including:
Writing samples for discussion
Pages for student practice

**Written by
Judith S. Gould
&
Mary F. Burke**

Illustrated by Ron Wheeler

Teaching & Learning Company

1204 Buchanan St., P.O. Box 10
Carthage, IL 62321-0010

This book belongs to

_____

Cover design by Sara King

Copyright © 2005, Teaching & Learning Company

ISBN No. 1-57310-471-X

Printing No. 987654321

Teaching & Learning Company
1204 Buchanan St., P.O. Box 10
Carthage, IL 62321-0010

Table of Contents

©2005 Teaching & Learning Company. Permission granted to reproduce this page for classroom use only.

Dear Teacher or Parent,

In our collective experience, we've found lots of instructional writing books that have told teachers to include lessons on style. They've even identified the elements of style, but they omit the samples and activities for teachers to use. That's hours and hours of finding models and designing exercises for students. That's time teachers just don't have anymore.

This book not only explains the elements of style, but models them and provides scaffolded practice for your students. We recommend that you do these activities in the order presented. You will find that the activities also work independently, if you would prefer to present them out of order. After practicing each skill, encourage your students to apply them in their own writing. The last section of this book includes story skeletons for application of some or all of the skills.

We know this book will provide you with a practical resource for writing instruction so you can coach your students to gold medal writing!

Sincerely,

Judith   Mary

Judith S. Gould and Mary F. Burke

TLC10471 Copyright © Teaching & Learning Company, Carthage, IL 62321-00

Elaboration

It's All in the Details

Coach's Playbook
Elaboration

Here's a good news/bad news joke.

Let's start with the bad news: Of all the elements of writing, elaboration is probably the most difficult to teach.

Just what you wanted to hear, wasn't it?

Now for the good news: The following pages were created to make it easy for you.

Elaboration is all about the details—which to include and how to make them interesting on paper. The Elaboration section in this book is the largest because elaboration requires a great deal of practice. And we certainly have provided you with a ton of it!

The practice pages begin with having students identify the different elements of elaboration. The next exercises require them to practice elaboration at an easy level, where students only give one small piece of extension. These practice pages build slowly to develop complete elaboration, where students have to provide all the details in a paragraph.

The Teacher's Reference Pages are provided with a running commentary on the paragraph's elaboration so you can understand the elements easily.

We believe using the models and the practice will help your students understand the elements of elaboration and their importance to strong writing. Continued practice will transform thin and mediocre writing into writing that is authentically powerful.

Elaboration 1

Leaving out ELABORATION is like striking out on your first at bat. You've got nothing. In order to score BIG with your writing, you've got to SEE it clearly.

Include: S—Supporting detail
           E—Example
           E—Extension

ELABORATION

In the following paragraph, the first sentence is the MAIN IDEA. The next sentence has SUPPORTING DETAIL. The third sentence is the EXAMPLE. All the sentences that follow extend the example; they are the EXTENSION. They tell more about the example.

My brother is quite annoying. He never leaves me alone. He follows me wherever I go. While he follows me, he also mimics everything I do and say. If I go outside and climb our jungle gym, he's out there like my shadow doing the same thing. If I'm talking to my friends on the phone, he'll say exactly what I'm saying but in a louder voice. I'm thinking of not showering for a couple of days to see if my terrible body odor will keep him away.

KEEP YOUR EYE ON THE BALL! Can you SEE it? Read the next paragraph. Then underline the MAIN IDEA. Circle the SUPPORTING DETAIL. Put a dotted line under the EXAMPLE. Draw a box around the EXTENSION.

My grandmother is not like any other grandmother I know. She is unique because, even for a 79-year-old woman, she is fearless. She rides a Harley™ cross-country every summer to visit us. That's over a thousand miles by herself. Every birthday since her 70th, she has bungee jumped off a nearby bridge in Eugene, Oregon, where she lives. She says it keeps her feeling young.

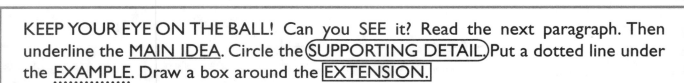

Elaboration 1
Scorecard

ANSWERS

KEEP YOUR EYE ON THE BALL! Can you SEE it? Read the next paragraph. Then underline the <u>MAIN IDEA</u>. Circle the SUPPORTING DETAIL. Put a dotted line under the EXAMPLE. Draw a box around the EXTENSION.

<u>My grandmother is not like any other grandmother I know.</u> She is unique because,
This is the main idea of this paragraph.   *This is the supporting*

even for a 79-year-old woman, she is fearless. She rides a Harley™ cross-country
detail because it is about the main idea.   *This is more information about the*

every summer to visit us. That's over a thousand miles by herself. Every birthday since
supporting detail—like proof.   *Even more information about her trip.*

her 70th, she has bungee jumped off a nearby bridge in Eugene, Oregon, where she
This is more information that proves the supporting detail.

lives. She says it keeps her feeling young.
           This ties up the paragraph.

When you build more detail on a simple example, you are elaborating. In order to score BIG with your writing, you've got to SEE how to elaborate it clearly.

Include: S—Supporting detail
E—Example
E—Extension

In the following paragraph, the first sentence is the MAIN IDEA. The next sentence has SUPPORTING DETAIL. The third sentence is the EXAMPLE. All the sentences that follow extend the example; they are the EXTENSION. They tell more about the example.

Visiting my grandmother's house is always fun. She has this amazing attic with the most interesting stuff in it. In the corner is a giant leather trunk covered in dust. Inside there are newspapers from the 1920s and 1930s. Under the newspapers are wooden toys, like tops and trucks of every size and shape. They're worn smooth as if they have been played with by hundreds of kids. I always wonder who those kids were that played with those toys.

KEEP YOUR EYE ON THE BALL! Can you SEE it? Read the next paragraph. Then underline the MAIN IDEA. Circle the SUPPORTING DETAIL. Put a dotted line under the EXAMPLE. Draw a box around the EXTENSION.

My dog Mel is an interesting creature. He enjoys making our cat Ripley crazy. He likes to chase Ripley around the house, but not all the time. Most days, Mel takes long, leisurely naps and barely notices Ripley at all. Then there are days when Mel pops up like a jack-in-the-box and chases Ripley like a mad dog. She never knows when or where Mel will do it. No wonder she always looks so nervous around him!

ANSWERS

KEEP YOUR EYE ON THE BALL! Can you SEE it? Read the next paragraph. Then underline the MAIN IDEA. Circle the SUPPORTING DETAIL. Put a dotted line under the EXAMPLE. Draw a box around the EXTENSION.

My dog Mel is an interesting creature. (He enjoys making our cat Ripley crazy.) He likes

This sentence is the main idea.   *This is the supporting detail.*

to chase Ripley around the house, but not all the time. Most days, Mel takes long,

This sentence is an example of the supporting detail.

leisurely naps and barely notices Ripley at all. Then there are days when Mel pops up

Now this is more information about the example—it tells about Mel's usual habits.

like a jack-in-the-box and chases Ripley like a mad dog. She never knows when or

Then it describes him with a simile—again, more information.   *More information about Ripley*

where Mel will do it. No wonder she always looks so nervous around him!

to add to the paragraph.   *This sentence ties it all up!*

Elaboration 3

Don't make your readers wonder what you mean—tell them with elaboration. In order to score BIG with your writing, you've got to SEE how to elaborate it clearly.

Include: S—Supporting detail
E—Example
E—Extension

©2005 Teaching & Learning Company. Permission granted to reproduce this page for classroom use only.

In the following paragraph, the first sentence is the MAIN IDEA. The next sentence has SUPPORTING DETAIL. The third sentence is the EXAMPLE. All the sentences that follow extend the example; they are the EXTENSION. They tell more about the example.

My room is my favorite place in the house. It's comfortable because all the things I adore are there. The walls, of course, are the color of Bazooka Bubble Gum™ because pink is my favorite color. On the wall I have posters of the movies I love and have seen dozens of times. There is a huge poster of the movie *The Return of the King* with Frodo in the middle of it. I fall asleep dreaming of hobbits every night.

KEEP YOUR EYE ON THE BALL! Can you SEE it? Read the next paragraph. Then underline the MAIN IDEA. Circle the SUPPORTING DETAIL. Put a dotted line under the EXAMPLE. Draw a box around the EXTENSION.

My friend Pat is my best friend. She is so helpful. Whenever I'm stuck in math, she'll come over and show me exactly what's wrong. I remember one time when I was learning multiplication, I was forgetting to carry some numbers. She showed me over and over until I got it right. It took over an hour and she never left my side until I understood it completely. Now that's a good friend!

Elaboration 3
Scorecard

ANSWERS

KEEP YOUR EYE ON THE BALL! Can you SEE it? Read the next paragraph. Then underline the <u>MAIN IDEA</u>. Circle the (SUPPORTING DETAIL). Put a dotted line under the EXAMPLE. Draw a box around the EXTENSION.

<u>My friend Pat is my best friend.</u> (She is so helpful.) Whenever I'm stuck in math, she'll
      This is the main idea.   *Supporting detail.*   *This is an example of*

come over and show me exactly what's wrong. I remember one time when I was
supporting detail—it's like proof.   *This tells about a specific time with*

learning multiplication, I was forgetting to carry some numbers. She showed me over
a specific task when Pat helped me.   *This sentence tells*

and over until I got it right. It took over an hour and she never left my side until I
exactly what she did to help me, and the following sentence tells how long she worked, which proves

understood it completely. Now that's a good friend!
that she is a helpful friend.

Elaboration 4

To extend something means to stretch or to reach. Remember to stretch your details when you write so you can reach your readers. In order to score BIG with your writing, you've got to SEE how to elaborate it clearly.

Include: S—Supporting detail
E—Example
E—Extension

In the following paragraph, the first sentence is the MAIN IDEA. The next sentence has SUPPORTING DETAIL. The third sentence is the EXAMPLE. All the sentences that follow extend the example; they are the EXTENSION. They tell more about the example.

When it comes to vacation, going to Disney World can't be beat. There are so many choices. There are four different parks in Disney World. My favorite is MGM Studios because they have fast action rides. My mom gets sick on the fast rides so she goes to Epcot where there's plenty of shopping and no rides to make her throw up her lunch.

KEEP YOUR EYE ON THE BALL! Can you SEE it? Read the next paragraph. Then underline the MAIN IDEA. Circle the (SUPPORTING DETAIL) Put a dotted line under the EXAMPLE. Draw a box around the EXTENSION.

My elderly aunt Martha has a perplexing personality. Sometimes the things she does make no sense to me at all. On one hand, she enjoys knitting and that kind of fits because of her age. On the other hand, she will only knit while watching action movies with plenty of explosions. Once she knit an entire sweater watching all the *Die Hard* movies.

Elaboration 4
Scorecard

KEEP YOUR EYE ON THE BALL! Can you SEE it? Read the next paragraph. Then underline the <u>MAIN IDEA</u>. Circle the (SUPPORTING DETAIL). Put a dotted line under the EXAMPLE. Draw a box around the EXTENSION.

<u>My elderly aunt Martha has a perplexing personality.</u> (Sometimes the things she does)

This is the main idea.   *This is the supporting detail*

(make no sense to me at all.) On one hand, she enjoys knitting and that kind of fits

of the main idea.   *Here is the beginning of the specific example that*

because of her age. On the other hand, she will only knit while watching action movies

confuses the writer.   *Here is the real source of the confusion because it doesn't go with*

with plenty of explosions. Once she knit an entire sweater watching all the *Die Hard*

being old and knitting.   *Here is the specific information about the kind of action movies that*

movies.

accompany her knitting.

t takes some thought to elaborate. You have to decide which details to include and which to leave out. In order to core BIG with your writing, you've got to SEE how to elaborate it clearly.

nclude: S—Supporting detail
E—Example
E—Extension

In the following paragraph, the first sentence is the MAIN IDEA. The next sentence has SUPPORTING DETAIL. The third sentence is the EXAMPLE. All the sentences that follow extend the example; they are the EXTENSION. They tell more about the example.

My cat can really be a pain in the neck. Lately, he has given up any kind of feeding schedule. He has decided that he will eat whenever he wants. If I am asleep, he finds ways to wake me up. The other night a noise happened when I was asleep that sounded something like skeletons dancing. Figaro had run his paw across the blinds because he was hungry. When I didn't get out of bed, he did it again and again. He's lucky I love him.

KEEP YOUR EYE ON THE BALL! Can you SEE it? Read the next paragraph. Then underline the MAIN IDEA. Circle the SUPPORTING DETAIL. Put a dotted line under the EXAMPLE. Draw a box around the EXTENSION.

My family is crazy about Walt Disney World. We even have a room in our house dedicated to Disney souvenirs. On the wall we have posters, tickets, pictures and banners from all of the Disney parks. The best part of the room is the doorway. We had a carpenter do a carving that includes Mickey, Minnie, Goofy and Donald. In the middle it says "The Disney Room." I guess I could say we are a little obsessed.

ANSWERS

KEEP YOUR EYE ON THE BALL! Can you SEE it? Read the next paragraph. Then underline the <u>MAIN IDEA</u>. Circle the (SUPPORTING DETAIL) Put a dotted line under the EXAMPLE. Draw a box around the EXTENSION.

<u>My family is crazy about Walt Disney World.</u> (We even have a room in our house ded-)
This is the main idea.   *I'm offering a piece of supporting*

(icated to Disney souvenirs.) On the wall we have posters, tickets, pictures and banners
detail here—proof.   *This example can better help my reader understand*

from all of the Disney parks. The best part of the room is the doorway. We had a car-
what the trinkets are.   *Now I've really extended it with specific details.*

penter do a carving that includes Mickey, Minnie, Goofy and Donald. In the middle it
Something the reader can SEE.

says "The Disney Room." I guess I could say we are a little obsessed.
Paragraph closing.

Elaboration 6

An example is a specific observation or event that proves the statement you make in your main idea sentence. Providing a clear, solid example is an important part of elaboration. In order to score BIG with your writing, you've got to SEE how to elaborate it clearly.

Include: S—Supporting detail
E—Example
E—Extension

ELABORATION

In the following paragraph, the first sentence is the MAIN IDEA. The next sentence has SUPPORTING DETAIL. The third sentence is the EXAMPLE. All the sentences that follow extend the example; they are the EXTENSION. They tell more about the example.

My sister Natalie really loves baseball. She has been a fan since our parents placed the first baseball cap on her delicate, little infant head. She never misses a game with her favorite team. In fact, she took a job working at Yankee Stadium to make sure she would be at every home game. Nat goes up and down the aisles yelling, "Peanuts! Get your peanuts here!" Working at home games and watching the away games on TV, she hasn't missed a game in 16 years.

KEEP YOUR EYE ON THE BALL! Can you SEE it? Read the next paragraph. Then underline the <u>MAIN IDEA</u>. Circle the (SUPPORTING DETAIL) Put a dotted line under the EXAMPLE. Draw a box around the EXTENSION.

ELABORATION

Bread is delicious but it isn't the easiest thing to bake. A bread baker has to be careful in measuring ingredients. Too much or too little of any ingredient can ruin the loaf. Once when baking, I became distracted and switched the amounts of yeast and sugar. This was a pretty sweet recipe; it called for 1/2 cup of sugar. When I added 1/2 cup of yeast and 1 tablespoon of sugar, a strange thing happened. The bread looked like something out of a horror movie!

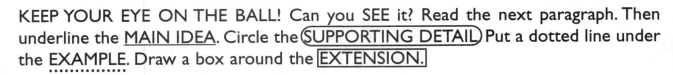

ANSWERS

KEEP YOUR EYE ON THE BALL! Can you SEE it? Read the next paragraph. Then underline the <u>MAIN IDEA</u>. Circle the (SUPPORTING DETAIL) Put a dotted line under the EXAMPLE. Draw a box around the EXTENSION.

<u>Bread is delicious but it isn't the easiest thing to bake.</u> (A bread baker has to be care-

This is the main idea. *This is the supporting*

(ful in measuring ingredients.) Too much or too little of any ingredient can ruin the loaf.

detail I have added. *Now, this example tells more about measuring, proving it is important.*

Once when baking, I became distracted and switched the amounts of yeast and sugar.

The extension by personal experience, a horror story from my kitchen, helps the reader SEE what could

This was a pretty sweet recipe; it called for ½ cup of sugar. When I added ½ cup of

happen. My extension reaches through the end of the paragraph.

yeast and I tablespoon of sugar, a strange thing happened. The bread looked like

something out of a horror movie!

Elaboration 7

When you write the main idea sentence, make sure you have an example to prove it and supporting details to back it up. In order to score BIG with your writing, you've got to SEE how to elaborate it clearly.

Include: S—Supporting detail
E—Example
E—Extension

In the following paragraph, the first sentence is the MAIN IDEA. The next sentence has SUPPORTING DETAIL. The third sentence is the EXAMPLE. All the sentences that follow extend the example; they are the EXTENSION. They tell more about the example.

My mom really likes Chinese food. We enjoyed Chinese cuisine quite often when I was a kid. It wasn't only once a week, either. Once on a family vacation, we were looking for a place to have dinner. We were in Washington, D.C., which certainly has some great restaurants. Mom wanted Chinese food, of course. She rolled down the window, followed her nose and told my dad to turn left at the next light. Leung's Kitchen had some of the best egg rolls I'd ever eaten. Good thing my mom had such a well-trained nose!

KEEP YOUR EYE ON THE BALL! Can you SEE it? Read the next paragraph. Then underline the <u>MAIN IDEA</u>. Circle the (SUPPORTING DETAIL) Put a dotted line under the EXAMPLE. Draw a box around the EXTENSION.

Nothing relaxes me more than a day at the beach. I can fill several hours lying on the sand. I usually bring a lot of books. On Sundays I bring my friends, and we play volleyball and swim all afternoon. Surrounded by breezes and the sound of the waves, I love to sink my toes into the sand and just watch the waves roll onto the beach. I'm glad I live near the shore.

Elaboration 7
Scorecard

KEEP YOUR EYE ON THE BALL! Can you SEE it? Read the next paragraph. Then underline the MAIN IDEA. Circle the SUPPORTING DETAIL. Put a dotted line under the EXAMPLE. Draw a box around the EXTENSION.

Nothing relaxes me more than a day at the beach. I can fill several hours lying on the
It's all about this.   *Proving that I must really like it there—*
sand. I usually bring a lot of books. On Sundays I bring my friends, and we play vol-
support. This example shows how I fill the hours.   *Extension: Information specific enough that my reader*
leyball and swim all afternoon. Surrounded by breezes and the sound of the waves, I
can SEE me there doing this.   *More specifics.*
love to sink my toes into the sand and just watch the waves roll onto the beach. I'm

glad I live near the shore.
Connecting personally with topic to close.

Elaboration 8

...ich people have a lot of money. This allows them to enjoy many interesting experiences and to own many things. Rich ...riting has a lot of detail. This allows the reader to enjoy many interesting experiences that the writer has described, ...nd to imagine what it would be like to own the life that the writer describes. In order to score BIG with your writ-...g, you've got to SEE how to elaborate it clearly.

...clude: S—Supporting detail
　　　　　E—Example
　　　　　E—Extension

ELABORATION

In the following paragraph, the first sentence is the MAIN IDEA. The next sentence has SUPPORTING DETAIL. The third sentence is the EXAMPLE. All the sentences that follow extend the example; they are the EXTENSION. They tell more about the example.

My good friend Tomas is really into dental health. Sometimes being around him can make me feel unclean. One time we went on a school trip together, and he was upset because he had forgotten something important from home. We went from store to store searching for a tongue scraper. I had never heard of such a thing. Tomas uses his every day! We discovered that these things are hard to find. The one store that carried them only had a battery-powered "turbo scraper." He had the best-kept mouth in the whole group!

ELABORATION

KEEP YOUR EYE ON THE BALL! Can you SEE it? Read the next paragraph. Then underline the <u>MAIN IDEA</u>. Circle the (SUPPORTING DETAIL.) Put a dotted line under the EXAMPLE. Draw a box around the EXTENSION.

My Aunt Shirley really holds our family together. She keeps in contact with everyone. I talk to her every Sunday and give her an update of events in my house. My sister talks to her weekly, too. One Sunday when I got off the phone with Aunt Shirley, my sister Deborah called. Deb lives only two miles away from me. When I said "hello," Deb asked when my chicken would be ready. Aunt Shirley, 1000 miles away, had already told her what we were having for dinner that night!

Elaboration 8
Scorecard

KEEP YOUR EYE ON THE BALL! Can you SEE it? Read the next paragraph. Then underline the <u>MAIN IDEA</u>. Circle the (SUPPORTING DETAIL.) Put a dotted line under the <u>EXAMPLE</u>. Draw a box around the [EXTENSION.]

<u>My Aunt Shirley really holds our family together.</u> (She keeps in contact with everyone.)
It's all about Aunt Shirley's powers.   *This tells how she does it—support.*

I talk to her every Sunday and give her an update of events in my house. [My sister]
An example of the ways that Aunt Shirley holds us together: once weekly.

[talks to her weekly, too.] One Sunday when I got off the phone with Aunt Shirley, my
This extension, shows that distance is no match for Aunt Shirley.

sister Deborah called. Deb lives only two miles away from me. When I said "hello,"
Specific information helping my reader to SEE that she can keep us close. Even though she was so

[Deb asked when my chicken would be ready.] Aunt Shirley, 1000 miles away, had already
far away, she was responsible for us dining together that night.

[told her what we were having for dinner that night!]
Can you SEE it?

Coach's Playbook
Elaboration Practice 1

One way to help your students understand the importance of detail is to gradually build their confidence with scaffolded levels of practice. Think of it as focusing on one muscle group at a time.

The following pages will provide practice with just EXTENSION. The MAIN IDEA, SUPPORTING DETAIL and EXAMPLE are provided. All your students have to do is to create EXTENSIONS that develop the writing.

Here is an example:

My favorite meal is spaghetti and meatballs. It is so much fun to eat. I love to play with my food, and I'm allowed to do it when I eat spaghetti.

_____

_____

_____

_____

_____

The example may be completed this way by adding an EXTENSION:

My favorite meal is spaghetti and meatballs. It is so much fun to eat. I love

to play with my food, and I'm allowed to do it when I eat spaghetti.

Noodles slurp and smack against my lips when I eat them. Twirling pasta

on my fork can keep me entertained for the entire meal. I even made up

a song about a meatball that rolled off my plate. I could eat

spaghetti every day for a year and never be bored.

Elaboration Practice 1A

Time to warm up your ELABORATION skills!

In the examples below, the paragraph provides you with a main idea, supporting detail and an example. You must writ the extension. All you have to do is add interesting information, like details that answer specifically WHO, WHA WHEN, WHERE or HOW. You'll knock this one out of the park!

ELABORATION

A beach picnic is the best. Food always tastes great outdoors. We always bring the grill.

_____

_____

_____

_____

_____

_____

There's nothing better than ice cream in the summer. It cools me off instantly. The

minute I take a bite, my mouth feels like it's entered a deep freeze. _____

_____

_____

_____

_____

_____

ELABORATION

Elaboration Practice 1B

Time to warm up your ELABORATION skills!

the examples below, the paragraph provides you with a main idea, supporting detail and an example. You must write e extension. All you have to do is add interesting information, like details that answer specifically WHO, WHAT, HEN, WHERE or HOW. You'll knock this one out of the park!

ELABORATION

Sleepovers are the most fun. My friends and I stay up late and get silly. Sometimes we pull tricks on one another. _____

_____

_____

_____

_____

_____

Visiting relatives can be weird. Sometimes I feel strange staying at someone else's house. Their daily routines are different. _____

_____

_____

_____

_____

_____

_____

ELABORATION

Coach's Playbook
Elaboration Practice 2

Now it's time to practice EXAMPLE and EXTENSIONS. The MAIN IDEA and SUPPORTING DETAIL are already provided. All your students have to do is to create EXAMPLES and EXTENSIONS that develop the writing.

Here is an example:

My favorite meal is spaghetti and meatballs. It is so much fun to eat.

_____

_____

_____

_____

_____

The example may be completed this way by adding an EXAMPLE and EXTENSIONS. Compare it to the paragraph on page 23.

My favorite meal is spaghetti and meatballs. It is so much fun to eat. I love to play with my food, and I'm allowed to do it when I eat spaghetti. Noodles slurp and smack against my lips when I eat them. Twirling pasta on my fork can keep me entertained for the entire meal. I even made up a song about a meatball that rolled off my plate. I could eat spaghetti every day for a year and never be bored.

TLC10471 Copyright © Teaching & Learning Company, Carthage, IL 62321-0

Elaboration Practice 2A

Time to warm up your ELABORATION skills!
In the examples below, the paragraph provides you with a main idea and supporting detail. You must write an example and extensions. With all the practice you've had, I see a home run in your future!

ELABORATION

We should get a class pet. It would help us be more responsible. _____

_____

_____

_____

_____

_____

_____

A big test is coming up. I plan to study with my friends. _____

_____

_____

_____

_____

_____

Elaboration Practice 2B

Time to warm up your ELABORATION skills!
In the examples below, the paragraph provides you with a main idea and supporting detail. You must write an examp
and extensions. With all the practice you've had, I see a home run in your future!

ELABORATION

My friend, _____, is so funny. He/She is always telling jokes.

_____

_____

_____

_____

_____

_____

_____

My teacher is so strict. He/She has rules for everything. _____

_____

_____

_____

_____

_____

_____

_____

Coach's Playbook
Elaboration Practice 3

This is the last of the scaffolded levels of practice. The following pages will provide practice with SUPPORTING DETAIL, EXAMPLE and EXTENSIONS. The MAIN IDEA is already provided. After all the stretching, warm-up and drill practice, your students should be ready to hit it out of the park!

Here is an example:

My favorite meal is spaghetti and meatballs.

_____

_____

_____

_____

_____

_____

The example may be completed this way (by adding DETAIL, EXAMPLE and EXTENSIONS). Compare it to the paragraph on page 26.

My favorite meal is spaghetti and meatballs.

It is so much fun to eat. I love to play with my food, and I'm allowed to do it when I eat spaghetti. Noodles slurp and smack against my lips when I eat them. Twirling pasta on my fork can keep me entertained for the entire meal. I even made up a song about a meatball that rolled off my plate. I could eat spaghetti every day for a year and never be bored.

29

Elaboration Practice 3A

Time to warm up your ELABORATION skills!
In the examples below, the paragraph provides you with a main idea. You must write the supporting detail, example an
extensions. With all the practice you've had, I see a home run in your future!

ELABORATION

Television commercials are so annoying. _____

_____

_____

_____

_____

_____

_____

I'm so glad I have a place to go where I can think. _____

_____

_____

_____

_____

_____

_____

_____

ELABORATION

TLC10471 Copyright © Teaching & Learning Company, Carthage, IL 62321-0

Elaboration Practice 3B

me to warm up your ELABORATION skills!
the examples below, the paragraph provides you with a main idea. You must write the supporting detail, example and
tensions. With all the practice you've had, I see a home run in your future!

Homework is not my favorite thing in the world. _____

_____

_____

_____

_____

_____

_____

Recess is my favorite part of the day. _____

_____

_____

_____

_____

_____

_____

Vocabulary Muscle

Choosing the Right Words

TLC10471 Copyright © Teaching & Learning Company, Carthage, IL 62321-0

Coach's Playbook
Build Your Vocabulary Muscle

Overuse of the thesaurus can sometimes make your writing seem like it is on steroids: overpowering and inhuman. It is better to train your muscles in a natural way. Writing needs to be natural.

Making word choices and using specific vocabulary does not mean that you need to consult *Roget's* at every turn. On most occasions, the best word to use is a word that the writer already knows.

The following section has exercises designed to sensitize your students to the conscious use of vocabulary and language when writing. These exercises are for group discussion. Don't be surprised if student choices differ from those expected. Pointing out examples of over-use or under-use of vocabulary can help your students understand how to make appropriate and interesting word choices.

Answer Key to Vocabulary Muscle Activities
Build Your Vocabulary Muscle 1, page 34—Set B
Build Your Vocabulary Muscle 2, page 35—Set B
Build Your Vocabulary Muscle 3, page 36—Set A
Build Your Vocabulary Muscle 4, page 37—Set C

Build Your Vocabulary Muscle 1

Words are the muscle behind good writing. Use words that are too weak, and you won't get the job done. But we don want our writing to be too bulked up, either. Huge, clumsy words can get in the way of the flow of language.

Read the following paragraphs. One has good muscle tone; it is fit and working well. One is weak. Another is so heav you need a spotter to lift it. Which is best? Can you spot the one with just the right VOCABULARY MUSCLE? Be pre pared to defend your choice if there is a disagreement.

SET A

Enjoying the occasional coastal respite allows for many views that engage the visual sense. Scampering within the salinic hydration, one can spot a plethora of aquatic life forms. Shoreline aficiona-dos engage in ambulatory activities. Juvenile homo-sapiens frolic. Solar radiation engulfs my epidermis. The summation of my senso-ry experiences provide great pleasure.

SET B

The beach is a lovely place. The plentiful fish and other sea life are both colorful and fascinating to look at. Couples can enjoy a carefree stroll. Children laugh and play. At the shore, I soak up the warm, radiant sun on my skin. I truly love my time at the beach.

SET C

The beach is pretty. There's lots of stuff swimming in the water. People move around. The kids play. Sun shines on my skin. It makes me feel nice.

TLC10471 Copyright © Teaching & Learning Company, Carthage, IL 62321-00

Build Your Vocabulary Muscle 2

Words are the muscle behind good writing. Use words that are too weak, and you won't get the job done. But we don't want our writing to be too bulked up, either. Huge, clumsy words can get in the way of the flow of language.

Read the following paragraphs. One has good muscle tone; it is fit and working well. One is weak. Another is so heavy you need a spotter to lift it. Which is best? Can you spot the one with just the right VOCABULARY MUSCLE? Be prepared to defend your choice if there is a disagreement.

©2005 Teaching & Learning Company. Permission granted to reproduce this page for classroom use only.

SET A

On Sunday mornings I don't do much. Sometimes I read things. We eat good food. Otherwise we hang. Sundays are good.

SET B

Sunday mornings are a time to ignore the "to do" list. Sometimes I dig into a good book or watch an old movie. We eat hot bagels with mountains of cream cheese. Everyone goes for a walk in the afternoon. Sundays are the best.

SET C

In the antemeridian hours of the commencing day of the week, I generally disengage from productive activity. Occasionally I activate my literary proclivities or monitor nostalgic cinema. My repast is composed of quality ingredients. All parties participate in a pre-dusk constitutional. Sundays are most agreeable.

Build Your Vocabulary Muscle 3

Words are the muscle behind good writing. Use words that are too weak, and you won't get the job done. But we dor want our writing to be too bulked up, either. Huge, clumsy words can get in the way of the flow of language.

Read the following paragraphs. One has good muscle tone; it is fit and working well. One is weak. Another is so hea you need a spotter to lift it. Which is best? Can you spot the one with just the right VOCABULARY MUSCLE? Be pr pared to defend your choice if there is a disagreement.

SET A

To make a peanut butter and jelly sandwich, find a knife, plate, napkin, two slices of your favorite bread and, of course, the jars of peanut butter and jelly. Place one slice of bread on the plate. Gently dip the knife in the opened jar of peanut butter and scoop some out. Spread it liberally on the bread. Now dip the knife in the opened jar of jelly, scoop some out, and gently spread it across the top of the peanut butter. Place the other slice of bread on top of your creation and enjoy.

SET B

When you make a peanut butter and jelly sandwich you first need to get the stuff. Put it on the plate. Once the bread is on the plate put peanut butter on it. Put on jelly. Put it together.

SET C

In order to construct the optimal portable lunch, it is first necessary to obtain the required instruments. Be sure to use a serrated slicing and spreading utensil. Also obtain a container each full of the creamed particles of peanuts and the preserved sweetened fruit. The appropriate application of each ingredient will facilitate consumption. Each item must be layered on a leavened baked good and then carefully compacted.

TLC10471 Copyright © Teaching & Learning Company, Carthage, IL 62321-0

Build Your Vocabulary Muscle 4

Words are the muscle behind good writing. Use words that are too weak, and you won't get the job done. But we don't want our writing to be too bulked up, either. Huge, clumsy words can get in the way of the flow of language.

Read the following paragraphs. One has good muscle tone; it is fit and working well. One is weak. Another is so heavy you need a spotter to lift it. Which is best? Can you spot the one with just the right VOCABULARY MUSCLE? Be prepared to defend your choice if there is a disagreement.

SET A

To read music you look at the lines and dots. Count the beats. One mark tells you the note and the other marks tell you other things.

SET B

Deciphering musical annotations requires careful study of the recorded information. Horizontal inscriptions and the vacancies between them indicate pitch. Examining the qualities and dimensions of the note itself will enable the reader to comprehend the composer's intended duration of the note.

SET C

Reading music is easy if you know what each mark means. The lines from the bottom up are labeled e, g, b, d and f. Is your note on a line? Then it is one of these. The spaces, bottom to top, are f, a, c and e. Now that you can figure out the pitch, we need to find the rhythm. Is the note filled in or hollow? Hollow notes are generally held longer. Does the note have a stick on it? A flag? All of these things help a musician to know how long a note should be held.

Build Your Vocabulary Muscle
Batting Practice 1

Now that you have refined your scouting skills, you can spot a stinker when you see one. Well, the following piece i a stinker. Do what you can to fix it up with just the right amount of VOCABULARY MUSCLE. Rewrite it in the spac provided below.

To place a phone call the first thing one must undertake is the lifting of the aural receptacle from the cradle of the implement. Place said receptacle adjacent to your ear so that you can ascertain if it is primed for the procedure. Using the digits of either hand, depress the alpha-numeric keys in appropriate sequence until the series is completed. Placing the receiver beside ear and mouth, listen for a salutation indicating successful completion of the connection.

What was that all about? _____

Too much language or too little? _____

Fix it by rewriting it. Think about the words you use as you rework it.

_____

_____

_____

_____

_____

_____

_____

BATTING PRACTICE #1

Build Your Vocabulary Muscle
Batting Practice 2

Now that you have refined your scouting skills, you can spot a stinker when you see one. Well, the following piece is a stinker. Do what you can to fix it up with just the right amount of VOCABULARY MUSCLE. Rewrite it in the space provided below.

If you want to hit a baseball you need to hold the stick thing. Look at the ball when the dude throws it to you. If the throw stinks, let it go. Wait for a good one. Then whack the thing. Then run for it.

What was that all about? _____

Too much language or too little? _____

Fix it by rewriting it. Think about the words you use as you rework it.

_____

_____

_____

_____

_____

_____

_____

_____

BATTING PRACTICE #2

Build Your Vocabulary Muscle
Batting Practice 3

Now that you have refined your scouting skills, you can spot a stinker when you see one. Well, the following piece is stinker. Do what you can to fix it up with just the right amount of VOCABULARY MUSCLE. Rewrite it in the spac provided below.

My maternal grandmother could prepare a divine soup comprised of breast of fowl, enriched egg pasta and a vast selection of garden-grown delicacies. The preparation of this delight necessitated her early departure from her slumber chamber, in order to allow the fluids of the various ingredients the requisite melding time.

What was that all about? _____

Too much language or too little? _____

Fix it by rewriting it. Think about the words you use as you rework it.

_____

_____

_____

_____

_____

_____

_____

_____

_____

BATTING PRACTICE #3

TLC10471 Copyright © Teaching & Learning Company, Carthage, IL 62321-001

Build Your Vocabulary Muscle
Batting Practice 4

Now that you have refined your scouting skills, you can spot a stinker when you see one. Well, the following piece is a stinker. Do what you can to fix it up with just the right amount of VOCABULARY MUSCLE. Rewrite it in the space provided below.

It's easy to ride a bike. Hold those things at the top and sit on that part in the middle. Use your feet to push the bottom sections. Turn the front end right or left to steer. Be sure you wear something to protect your head.

What was that all about? _____

Too much language or too little? _____

Fix it by rewriting it. Think about the words you use as you rework it.

_____

_____

_____

_____

_____

_____

_____

_____

BATTING PRACTICE #3

Descriptivitis

Using Moderation in Description

Coach's Playbook
Descriptivitis

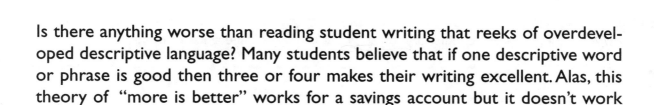

Is there anything worse than reading student writing that reeks of overdeveloped descriptive language? Many students believe that if one descriptive word or phrase is good then three or four makes their writing excellent. Alas, this theory of "more is better" works for a savings account but it doesn't work for writing. In writing, one well-chosen word is often better than two or three commonplace words.

The exercises that follow provide your students with an opportunity to discriminate among barely adequate descriptions, effective descriptive language and description that smothers interest.

The exercises are for group discussion. Don't be surprised if your students' selections are in error at first. Pointing out specific examples in the exercises will gradually help them develop proficient descriptive language.

Answer Key for Descriptivitis Activities
Descriptivitis 1, page 44—Set C
Descriptivitis 2, page 45—Set B
Descriptivitis 3, page 46—Set B
Descriptivitis 4, page 47—Set A

Descriptivitis 1

Descriptivitis is like a wild throw in baseball. A ball thrown with too little power or too much power doesn't get the job done. Skillful use of descriptive language in writing will pitch your words into the "strike zone" each and every time.

Read these three paragraphs. Only one includes descriptive language in the strike zone. The other two are foul! Can you spot the winner? Be prepared to defend your choice if there is a difference of opinion!

SET A

Saturday at my house is really extremely very busy. In the sunny mornings, Saturdays mean a vast and tremendous breakfast. My capable and gorgeous mom makes delicious and scrumptious waffles along with two kinds of yummy egg dishes, sizzling and spicy sausage and fresh ripened fruit. We all pitch in to help. I usually cut up the sweet and juicy strawberries and the special melon, and my sister makes toast in the most special way. After such an amazing breakfast, it's time for exhausting chores. My hardworking dad mows our gargantuan yard and trims the bushy hedges. My whining and complaining brothers clean out the unsightly and gross garage.

SET B

Saturday at my house is busy. Saturdays always mean a big breakfast. My mom makes waffles with some other dishes. We all help. I cut up strawberries and melon, and my sister makes the toast. After breakfast, it's time for some chores. My dad mows the yard and trims the hedges. My brothers clean out the garage.

SET C

Saturdays at my house are very energetic. In the mornings, Saturdays mean a hearty breakfast. My mom makes mouthwatering waffles along with two kinds of egg dishes and some fruit. We all pitch in to help. I usually cut up the strawberries and the fresh melon, and my younger sister makes the toast. After breakfast, it's time for chores. My dad mows the lawn and trims the hedges with the skill of a barber. My whiny brothers clean out the cluttered garage.

Descriptivitis 2

Descriptivitis is like a wild throw in baseball. A ball thrown with too little power or too much power doesn't get the job done. Skillful use of descriptive language in writing will pitch your words into the "strike zone" each and every time.

Read these three paragraphs. Only one includes descriptive language in the strike zone. The other two are foul! Can you spot the winner? Be prepared to defend your choice if there is a difference of opinion!

SET A

It was time for lunch. We grabbed our lunch boxes and our books to read. Our teacher told us to line up. We walked down the stairs to the cafeteria. The cafeteria was loud. We sat at a table. We opened our lunches and began to eat. We saw something. Walking in between tables, a dog wandered from table to table sniffing lunches.

SET B

Finally it was time for lunch. We grabbed our lunches and brought our books to read. Our teacher told us to line up in an orderly fashion. We walked noisily down the stairs into the crowded cafeteria. The cafeteria was as loud as a circus act. We sat down at a cleared table to start eating. Suddenly, we saw something. Walking in between tables, a mangy dog wandered casually about and began sniffing unattended lunches.

SET C

It was time for our fantastic and incredible lunch. We got our multicolored lunch boxes and our interesting and fascinating books to read. Our brilliant teacher told us to line up orderly and quietly. We walked noisily down the shiny and waxed stairs to our enormously gigantic cafeteria. Our vast cafeteria was as loud as a screaming party. We sat down at a pure and clean white table with miniature and tiny brown flecks all over it. We opened our delicious lunches and started eating hungrily. Suddenly, we saw something mysterious and delightful. Walking in between our fabulously clean tables, a mangy and scraggly dog wandered hungrily and began ferociously sniffing unattended lunches.

Descriptivitis 3

Descriptivitis is like a wild throw in baseball. A ball thrown with too little power or too much power doesn't get the job done. Skillful use of descriptive language in writing will pitch your words into the "strike zone" each and every time.

Read these three paragraphs. Only one includes descriptive language in the strike zone. The other two are foul! Can you spot the winner? Be prepared to defend your choice if there is a difference of opinion!

SET A

Tina's helpful mother drove her enthusiastic soccer team to the state championship tournament. She carefully stocked the family van with a variety and assortment of healthy and robust snacks before leaving their gorgeously decorated house. While the restless and high-strung athletes rode, they ate and chatted nervously about the upcoming critical and decisive game. Eating ferociously took their minds off their extensive and abundant nervousness.

SET B

Tina's mother drove her soccer team to the state tournament. She stocked the family van with a variety of healthy snacks before leaving the house. While the athletes rode, they ate and chatted anxiously about the upcoming game. Eating took their minds off their extreme nervousness.

SET C

Tina's mother drove her team to the tournament. She stocked the van with snacks before leaving the house. While the kids rode, they ate and chatted about the game. Eating took their minds off their nervousness.

Descriptivitis 4

Descriptivitis is like a wild throw in baseball. A ball thrown with too little power or too much power doesn't get the job done. Skillful use of descriptive language in writing will pitch your words into the "strike zone" each and every time.

Read these three paragraphs. Only one includes descriptive language in the strike zone. The other two are foul! Can you spot the winner? Be prepared to defend your choice if there is a difference of opinion!

SET A

The naughty child ran all through the empty room. Suddenly, he hid behind the overstuffed sofa and waited for the unsuspecting tabby cat to jump on top. He yelled, "Boo!" He laughed gleefully as he watched the astonished cat scamper nervously up the silk curtains in complete distress.

SET B

The naughty, awful and disobedient child ran all through the clean and empty room. Suddenly and without any warning at all, he hid behind the large and comfortable overstuffed sofa and waited for the massive, fluffy and unsuspecting tabby cat to jump on top. Abruptly, he yelled, "Boo!" Playfully and gleefully, he laughed like a hyena as he watched the distressed and astonished cat scamper nervously up the beautiful and silk curtains in utter and complete distress.

SET C

The child ran all through the room. He hid behind the sofa and waited for the cat to jump on top. He yelled, "Boo!" He laughed as he watched the cat scamper up the curtains.

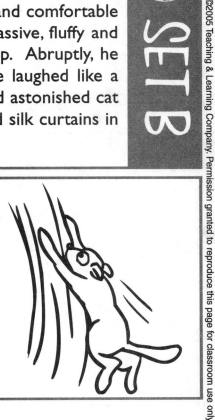

Build Your Vocabulary Muscle
Base Hit 1

Now that you have refined your scouting skills, you can spot a stinker when you see one. Well, the following piece a stinker. Do what you can to fix it up. Rewrite it in the space provided below.

 We left for the campgrounds early one gorgeous and brilliant Saturday morning. We packed our overstuffed car with all the important and essential camping equipment needed. Our massive van was also filled with bags of delicious and mouth-watering groceries that we would use on our extended 14-day camping trip. Before we left our lonely but carefully locked house, we checked the long and detailed list of necessary and important items. A successful and happy camping trip depends on being gloriously and stupendously prepared and ready.

Oh—it hurts just to read this! Fix it—quickly!

_____

_____

_____

_____

_____

_____

_____

_____

_____

BASE HIT 1

TLC10471 Copyright © Teaching & Learning Company, Carthage, IL 62321-001

Build Your Vocabulary Muscle
Base Hit 2

Now that you have refined your scouting skills, you can spot a stinker when you see one. Well, the following piece is a stinker. Do what you can to fix it up. Rewrite it in the space provided below.

The supreme and noble surfing contest was held on the glorious and pristine shores of Atlantic Beach. All the athletic and powerful participants arrived especially early to check out the unpredictable and unforeseen conditions of the vast and tremendous ocean. One by one, the dominant and commanding surfers took to the churning and overpowering waves. Many of them rode them mightily with fearlessness and grace while others faltered shamefully in wipeout after wipeout.

Oh—it hurts just to read this! Fix it—quickly!

_____

_____

_____

_____

_____

_____

_____

_____

_____

_____

BASE HIT 2

Build Your Vocabulary Muscle
Base Hit 3

Now that you have refined your scouting skills, you can spot a stinker when you see one. Well, the following piece a stinker. Do what you can to fix it up. Rewrite it in the space provided below.

My bodacious and courageous friend Gloria had a superb and rollicking birthday party. Her vast and meticulously decorated living room was covered with enormous multicolored balloons and dangling pastel streamers. Her brightly wrapped and shiny gifts sat on the polished oak table over by the sparkling clean windows. Outside in the beautifully mowed backyard, a jolly and giddy clown entertained the appreciative and stunned crowd with skillful and amazing feats of juggling.

Oh—it hurts just to read this! Fix it—quickly!

_____

_____

_____

_____

_____

_____

_____

_____

_____

BASE HIT 3

Build Your Vocabulary Muscle
Base Hit 4

Now that you have refined your scouting skills, you can spot a stinker when you see one. Well, the following piece is stinker. Do what you can to fix it up. Rewrite it in the space provided below.

The exciting and breathtaking soccer game proved most thrilling. The powerful and robust home team floundered in the pitiful first half executing many gruesome and awful errors. After the short but restful halftime period, the refreshed and renewed home team came out onto the muddy and rain-soaked field with a powerful and sharp attitude. They completed every play forcefully and quickly and by the end of the breathtaking game, they proved themselves perfectly and completely victorious.

Oh—it hurts just to read this! Fix it—quickly!

_____

_____

_____

_____

_____

_____

_____

_____

_____

BASE HIT 4

Dead Verbs

Burying Bad Habits

Coach's Playbook
Dead Verbs

Having the right word is more important than having the most words. And in many ways, verbs can do a better job describing than adjectives. Consider the following sentences:

The young, shiny, strong horse walked into the stable.

The horse pranced into the stable.

Or consider these:

The big, red, dented, rusted ship was in the harbor.

The ship rested in the harbor.

So, how do you get students to use more of these carefully chosen descriptive verbs? One way is to bury the "dead" verbs. The following page lists all the help-ing (dead) verbs. Introduce these verbs to your students using the following pro-cedure. First ask students what verbs do. Invariably, they will tell you that verbs are action words. Then hand out the "Act Out a Verb" cards to your students. Ask for volunteers to act out the verbs, as in a charades game. The others can try to guess the verbs. When the acting is done, the ones still holding cards can "bury" them. Why not bring along a shovel and actually go through with it?

Then, in remembrance of the "dearly departed" verbs, give each student a copy of the page listing each one. Have your students memorize the DEAD VERBS. Once they know these verbs they can avoid using them in their writing! Then work with the writing samples in this section. Encourage your students to discuss the effects the powerful verbs had on the writing. Finally, complete the exercises for rewrit-ing passages that have been destroyed by over-use of dead verbs.

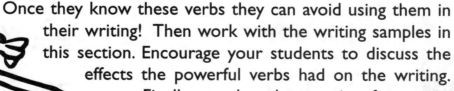

Dead Verbs

(Also known as Helping Verbs)

1. am
2. are
3. be
4. been
5. being
6. can
7. could
8. did
9. do
10. does
11. had
12. has

13. have
14. is
15. may
16. might
17. must
18. shall
19. should
20. was
21. were
22. will
23. would

TLC10471 Copyright © Teaching & Learning Company, Carthage, IL 62321-00

Reproducible
"Act Out a Verb" Cards

Act Out a Verb	Act Out a Verb	Act Out a Verb
AM	IS	ARE
Act Out a Verb	Act Out a Verb	Act Out a Verb
WAS	WERE	HAS
Act Out a Verb	Act Out a Verb	Act Out a Verb
HAVE	HAD	DO
Act Out a Verb	Act Out a Verb	Act Out a Verb
DOES	MIGHT	DID
Act Out a Verb	Act Out a Verb	Act Out a Verb
RUN	JUMP	DIG

Reproducible
"Act Out a Verb" Cards

Act Out a Verb	Act Out a Verb	Act Out a Verb
SING	**HOP**	**KICK**
Act Out a Verb	Act Out a Verb	Act Out a Verb
POINT	**KISS**	**BE**
Act Out a Verb	Act Out a Verb	Act Out a Verb
BEING	**BEEN**	**COULD**
Act Out a Verb	Act Out a Verb	Act Out a Verb
SHOULD	**STAND**	**DRINK**
Act Out a Verb	Act Out a Verb	Act Out a Verb
HUG	**SCRATCH**	**SPIN**

TLC10471 Copyright © Teaching & Learning Company, Carthage, IL 62321-0

R.I.P.

(Rotten in the Predicate)

Here lie dead verbs.
In life they did
almost nothing.

Dead Verbs Ball 1

Having too many DEAD VERBS in your sentences is like getting thrown out on a good hit. It stops the momentum. Look at the following two passages. In one, the ball is in the air, heading for the fence. In the other, it's a strikeout. Which is best? Can you spot the winner? Be prepared to defend your choice if there is a disagreement.

A The park is fabulous. There are trees. The birds are there, too. I can see the flowers. The grass is growing. I can feel it beneath my feet. The fresh air must be good for me.

B The park radiates a fabulous feeling of relaxation. Shade trees provide a cool resting place. Birds soar overhead. Flowers dot the landscape with vibrant color. Thick patches of grassy lawn cushion my every step. Each breath invigorates me.

Try these two. Which is best? Why is it best?

C Nothing matches the excitement of a great action movie. Suspense builds and every audience member's blood pressure rises, waiting for the climax. The heroes obliterate the villains. Body parts fly during bloody battle scenes. The hero triumphs.

D An action movie is fun. The movie has suspense. As it rises, so does the blood pressure of every audience member. The good guy has to beat up the bad guy. The bad guy has to lose. Sometimes there are flying body parts. The hero is the winner.

Dead Verbs Ball 2

Look at the following two passages. The first one strikes out with dead verbs. The second hits a home run with active verbs.

DEAD VERBS
My cat has orange fur. His ears are pointy. He can see me because he has eyes. His eyes are the same color as his fur. His tail is extra fluffy.

IT'S ALIVE!
An orange fuzz covers my cat's body. Triangular ears point out at the top. Round eyes gaze steadily into mine. Soft fluff covers his active, little tail.

You try. Get the DEAD VERBS out of the following example:

The roses are pretty. They are red. They have thorns. When I touch them I can feel them.

The thorns are really pointy. They are hurting me.

_____

_____

_____

_____

_____

Look at the following two passages. The first one strikes out with dead verbs. The second hits a home run with active verbs.

DEAD VERBS
I like ice cream. It has a good taste. I can get many different flavors.
I have a favorite. It is chocolate.

IT'S ALIVE!
Nothing tastes better than ice cream. Each flavor oozes a different blend of tempting sweets. Chocolate rocks.

You try. Get the DEAD VERBS out of the following example:

I have friends. After school we like to do things. Sports are a favorite. One thing I like is street hockey. It can be fun.

_____

_____

_____

_____

_____

_____

Show, Don't Tell

Using Action and Specificity to Develop a Topic

Coach's Playbook
Show, Don't Tell

Show, don't tell.

You've heard it a million times when it comes to good writing, but how in the world do you teach it to kids?

First of all, you need to understand it yourself in a way that makes sense and connects you to your prior knowledge. "Show, don't tell" is all about details that make a vivid and novel image in the reader's mind. It's also about using sensory images. It's about what you see, hear, taste, touch or smell. It's about cranking out action verbs and making them do the heavy lifting.

Example: The weather was lovely.

That's the telling, but it doesn't tell us much, does it? "Lovely" can be a lot of things to a lot of people. Now, here's how you SHOW instead of tell:

The sun <u>shone</u> down with gentle grace. The sky <u>completed</u> an azure blue border everywhere you looked. A light breeze <u>stirred</u> the fragrance of wildflowers sprouting in nearby yards.

Notice the active verbs present in those sentences. Active—not linking—verbs are crucial to "show, don't tell."

The following exercises are scaffolded from easier to more challenging practice. They were designed to give your students lots of experience with this very challenging concept.

Show, Don't Tell 1

Have you ever listened to a ball game on the radio? A good announcer won't just tell you that a home team scored a home run. The announcer will tell you that the batter bunted the ball, he made it to first base and the third-base runner slid into home plate. The batter had leaned into the pitch like he was really going to slug it out of the field, but at the last second he stepped back and dropped the ball short on the infield. While the catcher and the pitcher scrambled to retrieve the ball, the runner on third raced to home plate and slid to safety. The crowd went wild. Good radio announcers describe what they see so well that you can almost see it yourself. That is what we need to do as writers.

**EXAMPLE**

Here is an example of just TELLING:
    Grandpa loved music.
This is an example of SHOWING:
    Every time we visited Grandpa, he put on his 78-speed records. He strummed his ukulele and sang along. He knew every word to those old songs.

NOW YOU TRY

Here is an example of just TELLING:
    That meal was delicious.
Help your reader see it better by SHOWING. Use these questions to help you rewrite it to SHOW the reader.

1. What was the meal?   4. How many courses?
2. How was it served?   5. Who did the cooking?
3. What did you drink?   6. Tell about dessert.

_____

_____

_____

NOW YOU TRY

Here is an example of just TELLING:
    The ball game was exciting.
Help your reader see it better by SHOWING.

_____

_____

_____

_____

Show, Don't Tell 2

Have you ever listened to a ball game on the radio? A good announcer won't just tell you that a home team scored [a] home run. The announcer will tell you that the batter bunted the ball, he made it to first base and the third-base runner slid into home plate. The batter had leaned into the pitch like he was really going to slug it out of the field, but [at] the last second he stepped back and dropped the ball short on the infield. While the catcher and the pitcher scram[bled] to retrieve the ball, the runner on third raced to home plate and slid to safety. The crowd went wild. Good radi[o] announcers describe what they see so well that you can almost see it yourself. That is what we need to do as writer[s.]

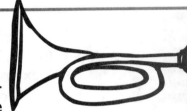

EXAMPLE

Here is an example of just TELLING:

The band was terrible.

This is an example of SHOWING:

The horn player blasted away in his own key, slightly different than the one used by the other musicians. When the singer took hold of the microphone she bellowed some notes lower than the bass played. The tempo changed frequently as the band slogged their way through the song.

NOW YOU TRY

Here is an example of just TELLING:

The roller coaster ride was fun.

Help your reader see it better by SHOWING. Use these questions to help you rewrite it to SHOW the reader.

1. How did the ride start?
2. How did people react?
3. How did the ride end?
4. How fast did it go?
5. What was the best part?
6. Would you do it again?

_____

_____

_____

_____

NOW YOU TRY

Here is an example of just TELLING:

My cat is pretty frisky.

Help your reader see it better by SHOWING.

_____

_____

_____

_____

TLC10471 Copyright © Teaching & Learning Company, Carthage, IL 62321-0[0]

Show, Don't Tell 3

Have you ever listened to a ball game on the radio? A good announcer won't just tell you that a home team scored a home run. The announcer will tell you that the batter bunted the ball, he made it to first base and the third-base runner slid into home plate. The batter had leaned into the pitch like he was really going to slug it out of the field, but at the last second he stepped back and dropped the ball short on the infield. While the catcher and the pitcher scrambled to retrieve the ball, the runner on third raced to home plate and slid to safety. The crowd went wild. Good radio announcers describe what they see so well that you can almost see it yourself. That is what we need to do as writers.

EXAMPLE

Here is an example of just TELLING:
   My friend Chris is nice.
This is an example of SHOWING:
   When I was sick with a cold, my friend Chris visited me and brought me my favorite books and magazines. Chris sat on the edge of my bed and read to me in goofy voices.

NOW YOU TRY

Here is an example of just TELLING:
   That basketball player is good.
Help your reader see it better by SHOWING. Use these questions to help you rewrite it to SHOW the reader.

1. Who is the player?
2. How does the player score?
3. How does the other team guard the player?
4. How does the player move to show skill?
5. How does the player defend the basket?

_____

_____

_____

_____

NOW YOU TRY

Here is an example of just TELLING:
   My mother is tired.
Help your reader see it better by SHOWING.

_____

_____

_____

_____

Show, Don't Tell 4

Have you ever listened to a ball game on the radio? A good announcer won't just tell you that a home team scored [a] home run. The announcer will tell you that the batter bunted the ball, he made it to first base and the third-base run ner slid into home plate. The batter had leaned into the pitch like he was really going to slug it out of the field, but [at] the last second he stepped back and dropped the ball short on the infield. While the catcher and the pitcher scram bled to retrieve the ball, the runner on third raced to home plate and slid to safety. The crowd went wild. Good rad[io] announcers describe what they see so well that you can almost see it yourself. That is what we need to do as writer[s.]

EXAMPLE

Here is an example of just TELLING:
> Saturdays are fun.

This is an example of SHOWING:
> On Saturdays, when I get up, my mother always makes me my favorite breakfast: French toast and bacon. Then we always swim at the pool before lunch. After lunch, I play my computer games for at least an hour.

NOW YOU TRY

Here is an example of just TELLING:
> Summer vacation is the best.

Help your reader see it better by SHOWING. Use these questions to help you rewrite it to SHOW the reader.

1. What do you do with your time?
2. Where do you go?
3. What is the best part?
4. Who do you spend time with?
5. How do you feel when it begins? Ends?

_____

_____

_____

_____

NOW YOU TRY

Here is an example of just TELLING:
> My room is a mess.

Help your reader see it better by SHOWING.

_____

_____

_____

_____

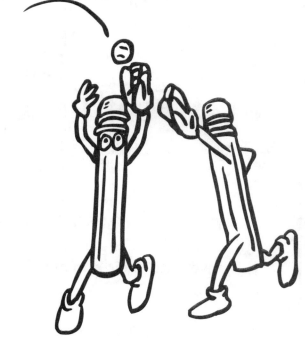

Fast Forward
& Slow Motion

Knowing What's Important in a Story and How to Pace the Action

Coach's Playbook
Fast Forward & Slow Motion

This section is all about figuring out what's important in a story. This is about critical thinking during writing. It is also about allowing students to be creative with their choices. This combination makes a challenging concept to teach.

Fast forward writing covers a span of time that is not essential to the story but must be mentioned for the sake of transitional time.

Here is an example:

> By the time we got to the
> ninth inning, the score was tied.

In this case, the writer doesn't need to go through all the details of the preceding innings, every at bat, every foul ball, every out—it doesn't matter to the story. Writers can fast forward to the important parts without having to tell every single detail that comes before the important part of a story.

The reason we fast forward is to get to the good part! When we get to the good part, the action should slow down so the reader can experience the details one at a time. Here is where word choice and effective description create pictures for the reader.

Answer Key to Practice Pages
Fast Forward & Slow Motion 1, page 70—Set B
Fast Forward & Slow Motion 2, page 71—Set C
Fast Forward & Slow Motion 3, page 72—Set B
Fast Forward & Slow Motion 4, page 73—Set A

TLC10471 Copyright © Teaching & Learning Company, Carthage, IL 62321-0

Coach's Playbook
Fast Forward & Slow Motion

Here is an example:

By the time we got to the ninth inning, the score was tied. Slowly, Mugs McMurphy sidled up to the plate. The crowd fell silent. Mugs hadn't

These are important details because this information will provide the reader with a

hit a ball all year. The first two pitches went by him. He never saw them.

feeling of suspense. The action is slowed down so the reader can be caught in the

Mugs dug his heels in the dirt, grabbed hold of the bat and steeled himself

hopelessness of the situation. The more the reader connects on an emotional

for the third pitch. The ball barreled toward him at 90mph with a wicked

level, the better the writing. More details here prolong the suspense and then

curve that broke just before the strike zone. He clobbered the ball

the writer gives the reader the payoff with a happy ending.

like a poisonous snake and stood there watching it soar out of the park. It was his only hit all year long.

Knowing when to use fast forward and slow motion writing is essential in developing a winning writing style.

The following practice pages are for group discussion. Students who talk about the elements of writing and can confidently discriminate between weak and strong pieces of prose will be able to internalize those characteristics in their own writing. They will be less dependent on you for that question that we know you love to hear: "Is this piece good?" With training and practice, they'll be able to answer that question themselves. Follow the italics for a running explanation for the writer's rationale for including the details.

Fast Forward & Slow Motion 1

A good coach can analyze the stats and call the right play at the right time. It can make or break a game. Timing is als[o] crucial to writing. Take too long on the build-up, and you've bored the audience. Sometimes it is better to FAST FOR[-]WARD through the less important information. But don't go too quickly through the good parts. Take time to revie[w] the SLOW MOTION of the important parts—slow the action in these sections to allow for description. Read the fo[l-]lowing paragraphs. Which is best? Can you spot the winner? Be prepared to defend your choice if there is a disagree[-]ment.

SET A

I went up the stairs. I walked down the hall. Step, step, step went my feet. Then I opened my door. After I opened it I went in. Then I closed the door. I sat on the bed and took off my slippers. Carefully, I pulled the covers down and slipped into my bed. Click! I reached over and turned out the light. That's when the monster jumped out of my closet.

SET B

I followed my usual bedtime routine that night. Up the stairs, into the bed and turn off the light. Then I thought I heard a noise. Click! I turned the light back on. I checked under the bed. Nothing. Behind the curtains. Coast was clear. I opened my closet. Everything looked normal, so I slid back into bed and turned off the light, but I heard it again. Click. Light back on. Then my closet door started opening. A shadowy figure emerged from behind my hanging clothes. A monster in my closet! A tall, green, hungry, kid-eating monster was staring down at me. After all the years of convincing myself that the stories were only fiction, they turned out to be true.

SET C

I followed my usual bedtime routine that night. Up the stairs, into the bed and turn off the light. That's when the monster jumped out of my closet.

good coach can analyze the stats and call the right play at the right time. It can make or break a game. Timing is also crucial to writing. Take too long on the build-up, and you've bored the audience. Sometimes it is better to FAST FORWARD through the less important information. But don't go too quickly through the good parts. Take time to review the SLOW MOTION of the important parts—slow the action in these sections to allow for description. Read the following paragraphs. Which is best? Can you spot the winner? Be prepared to defend your choice if there is a disagreement.

SET A

We landed front-row seats for the circus. Seeing all the animals and acrobats up close was incredible. It was pretty bad when the juggler dropped the flaming torch right into the crowd, though.

SET B

When we went to the circus we were supposed to be in row V, which would be 22 rows back from the center ring. Well, my sister Deb is kind of short, so we didn't want to be 22 rows back. She'd probably miss out on a lot of stuff. My neighbor works at the coliseum so she took our tickets to work one day and her boss exchanged them for better seats. When she told us they would be in the front row, we were very excited. After the 30-minute drive to the stadium, we parked and went inside. Dad stopped for popcorn and peanuts for everyone. We walked down the aisles: D, C, B, A. Right up front! During the show a juggler dropped a flaming torch right into the crowd. Ouch.

SET C

We landed front-row seats for the circus. Seeing all the animals and acrobats up close was incredible. One juggler had an amazing act. First he juggled expensive-looking plates three, four, five, six and then seven of these went flying in the air. He caught them all in a neat stack. Next he opened an unusual box and took out seven knives. When he threw them all in the air, I ducked because it was so close to where I sat. He juggled them flawlessly and they landed safely back into their box. For his finale, they dimmed the houselights. He used a lighter to ignite seven torches, and threw them in the air. Our faces burned with the heat of the dancing fires. Then it started getting warmer and warmer. The juggler had dropped a flaming torch into the front row, inches from my feet!

Fast Forward & Slow Motion 3

A good coach can analyze the stats and call the right play at the right time. It can make or break a game. Timing is als crucial to writing. Take too long on the build-up, and you've bored the audience. Sometimes it is better to FAST FOR WARD through the less important information. But don't go too quickly through the good parts. Take time to revie the SLOW MOTION of the important parts—slow the action in these sections to allow for description. Read the fo lowing paragraphs. Which is best? Can you spot the winner? Be prepared to defend your choice if there is a disagree ment.

SET A

I strolled upstairs to brush my teeth and wash my face. After I cleaned up and rinsed my mouth, I found my favorite pajamas—the ones with the sheep sleeping on fluffy clouds—and put them on. Deciding on a book to read was important, so I hemmed and hawed until I found my favorite, *Charlotte's Web* . After 20 minutes of reading, my eyes snapped shut and I fell fast asleep. Sometime well past midnight, a bright light startled me out of sleep. I got up and looked out the window. A small spacecraft had landed in my backyard. Two creatures came out and started towards our vegetable garden.

SET B

After my usual bedtime routine, I fell fast asleep. Sometime well past midnight, a bright light startled me out of my slumber. I looked out my window and saw a spaceship about the size of a doghouse hovering over the trees in our backyard. The purple fluorescent landing gears lowered. The craft landed without a sound. Racing out the door in seconds, I hid behind our BBQ grill watching the scene unfold. Two oddly shaped green creatures with large heads and bulging eyes emerged and began snipping the tomatoes, peppers and eggplant from my mother's vegetable garden.

SET C

After my usual bedtime routine, I fell fast asleep. Sometime well past midnight, a bright light startled me out of sleep. I got up and looked out the window. A small spacecraft had landed in my backyard. Two creatures came out and started toward our vegetable garden.

TLC10471 Copyright © Teaching & Learning Company, Carthage, IL 62321-00

A good coach can analyze the stats and call the right play at the right time. It can make or break a game. Timing is also crucial to writing. Take too long on the build-up, and you've bored the audience. Sometimes it is better to FAST FORWARD through the less important information. But don't go too quickly through the good parts. Take time to review the SLOW MOTION of the important parts—slow the action in these sections to allow for description. Read the following paragraphs. Which is best? Can you spot the winner? Be prepared to defend your choice if there is a disagreement.

SET A

The minute Mr. and Mrs. Smith left the house, their four-year-old twins, Zach and Jack, threw a 10-minute temper tantrum complete with kicking legs flailing fists and enough screeching to peel the paint off the walls. After that, they ran into the kitchen, grabbed the whipped cream and ketchup from the refrigerator and squirted everything in sight. Quick as I could, I scooped both weapons out of their hands, threw the bottles into the sink and led the boys to their playroom where all their damage could be contained in one place. Apparently they thought I was a human target because once we were in there, they threw every toy they had at me and didn't stop until they became tired and fell asleep. After putting them in bed, I relaxed and enjoyed my evening.

SET B

Baby-sitting the Smith twins has been the worst nightmare of my entire life. After putting them in bed, I relaxed and enjoyed my evening.

SET C

Baby-sitting the Smith twins has been the worst nightmare of my entire life. After putting them in bed, I relaxed and enjoyed my evening. The plasma TV had 150 channels programmed and I checked each one out. I got to see *Even Stevens* in Spanish! The Smith pantry overflowed with junk food of every variety, so I loaded up on chocolate cakes, fruit snacks and chips and dip. The Playstation™ was out and I spent the rest of the evening entertaining myself with that until the Smiths arrived home.

Varying
the
Game Plan
Sentence Variety

Coach's Playbook
Varying the Game Plan

It's 11:30 p.m. You're reading through a stack of student writing with your favorite late-night talk show host. You had assigned an essay to your students, and now it is your job to assess 32 papers on the merits of wearing seat belts.

You should wear them. You could get hurt. You might break a leg.
You might even crack your head. You can fly out of a window.
You can bump into things.

One after another after another. Countdown to sleep? You are not alone.

Repetitive sentence structures can take the life and style out of writing. Curing your students of this dreaded affliction can be as simple as explaining, modeling and practicing alternatives.

The following section contains two activities to help build varied, flowing sentences. The first, SLALOM SENTENCES, guides your students through scaffolded practices to create information-packed sentences. It is followed by exercises where variety is developed by sliding around different parts.

Another activity, the CURVE BALL, starts by modeling and providing practice for students to break sentences apart into subject, predicate and the phrase that tells how. Then a page is provided to practice using variety and an occasional CURVE BALL in sentence writing style.

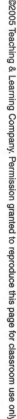

While there is no guarantee that student papers will automatically become so interesting that you are up for the late, late show, these strategies may help their sentences vary and flow.

Slalom Sentences 1

Sentences that sound repetitive and boring are like using the same batting lineup in every game. They're not only du
but when the other team sees what you're doing, you will lose your competitive edge. For variety in our writing, w
first need to build sentences that have some substance to them.

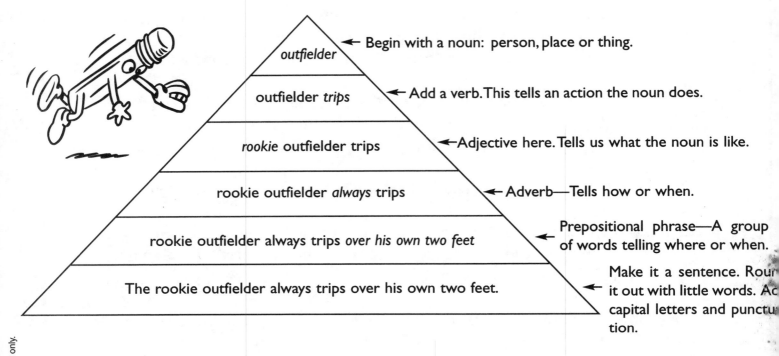

outfielder ← Begin with a noun: person, place or thing.

outfielder *trips* ← Add a verb. This tells an action the noun does.

rookie outfielder trips ←Adjective here. Tells us what the noun is like.

rookie outfielder *always* trips ← Adverb—Tells how or when.

rookie outfielder always trips *over his own two feet* ← Prepositional phrase—A group of words telling where or when.

The rookie outfielder always trips over his own two feet. ← Make it a sentence. Roun it out with little words. Ad capital letters and punctu tion.

Now you try one. You only need to add the prepositional phrase (where or when) and finish the sentence.

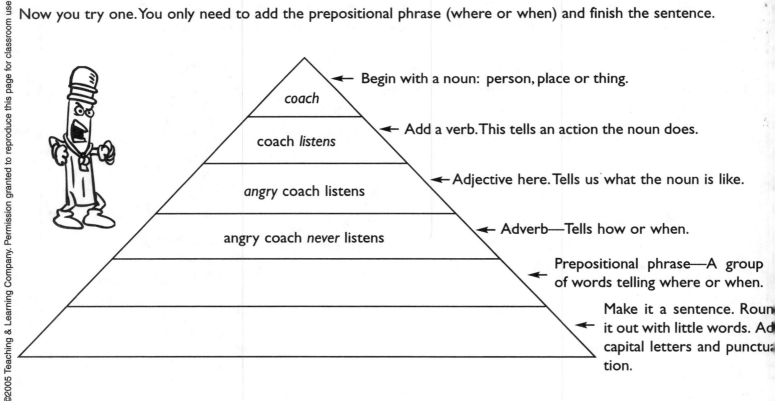

coach ← Begin with a noun: person, place or thing.

coach *listens* ← Add a verb. This tells an action the noun does.

angry coach listens ←Adjective here. Tells us what the noun is like.

angry coach *never* listens ← Adverb—Tells how or when.

← Prepositional phrase—A group of words telling where or when.

← Make it a sentence. Roun it out with little words. Ad capital letters and punctua tion.

Slalom Sentences 2

ntences that sound repetitive and boring are like using the same batting lineup in every game. They're not only dull, ut when the other team sees what you're doing, you will lose your competitive edge. For variety in our writing, we rst need to build sentences that have some substance to them.

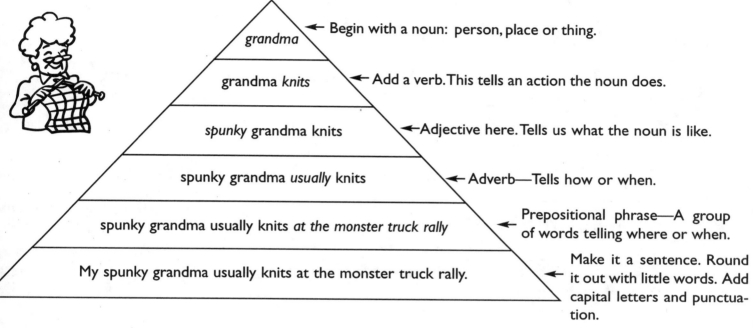

grandma ← Begin with a noun: person, place or thing.

grandma *knits* ← Add a verb. This tells an action the noun does.

spunky grandma knits ← Adjective here. Tells us what the noun is like.

spunky grandma *usually* knits ← Adverb—Tells how or when.

spunky grandma usually knits *at the monster truck rally* ← Prepositional phrase—A group of words telling where or when.

My spunky grandma usually knits at the monster truck rally. ← Make it a sentence. Round it out with little words. Add capital letters and punctuation.

low you try one. You only need to add the adverb (telling how or when), the prepositional phrase (where or when) d finish the sentence.

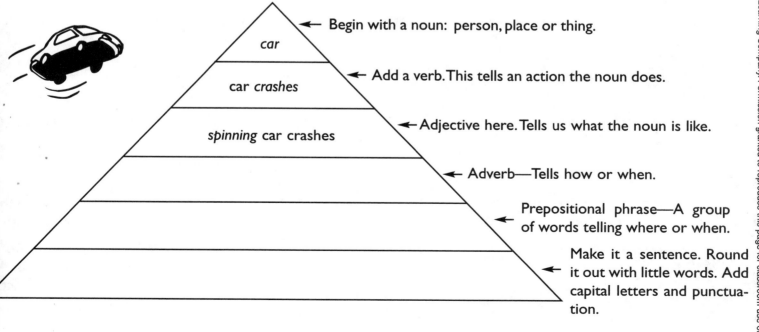

car ← Begin with a noun: person, place or thing.

car *crashes* ← Add a verb. This tells an action the noun does.

spinning car crashes ← Adjective here. Tells us what the noun is like.

← Adverb—Tells how or when.

← Prepositional phrase—A group of words telling where or when.

← Make it a sentence. Round it out with little words. Add capital letters and punctuation.

Slalom Sentences 3

Sentences that sound repetitive and boring are like using the same batting lineup in every game. They're not only du~~ll~~
but when the other team sees what you're doing, you will lose your competitive edge. For variety in our writing, w~~e~~
first need to build sentences that have some substance to them.

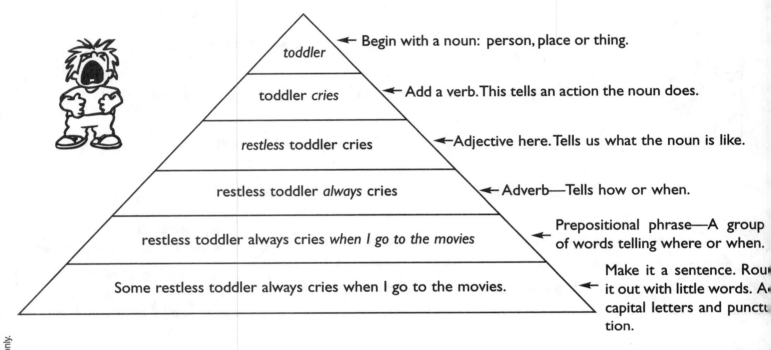

toddler ← Begin with a noun: person, place or thing.

toddler *cries* ← Add a verb. This tells an action the noun does.

restless toddler cries ← Adjective here. Tells us what the noun is like.

restless toddler *always* cries ← Adverb—Tells how or when.

restless toddler always cries *when I go to the movies* ← Prepositional phrase—A group of words telling where or when.

Some restless toddler always cries when I go to the movies. ← Make it a sentence. Rou~~nd~~ it out with little words. A~~dd~~ capital letters and punctu~~a~~tion.

Now you try one. You need to add an adjective (describing the noun), an **adverb** (telling how or when), the prepo~~si~~tional phrase (where or when) and finish the sentence.

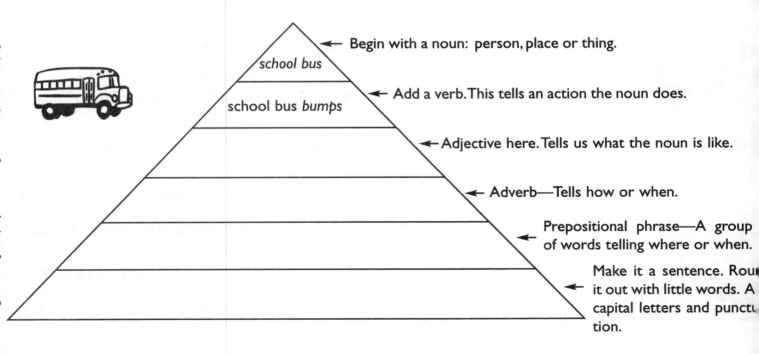

school bus ← Begin with a noun: person, place or thing.

school bus *bumps* ← Add a verb. This tells an action the noun does.

← Adjective here. Tells us what the noun is like.

← Adverb—Tells how or when.

← Prepositional phrase—A group of words telling where or when.

← Make it a sentence. Rou~~nd~~ it out with little words. A~~dd~~ capital letters and punctu~~a~~tion.

TLC10471 Copyright © Teaching & Learning Company, Carthage, IL 62321-0~~

Slalom Sentences 4

entences that sound repetitive and boring are like using the same batting lineup in every game. They're not only dull, ut when the other team sees what you're doing, you will lose your competitive edge. For variety in our writing, we rst need to build sentences that have some substance to them.

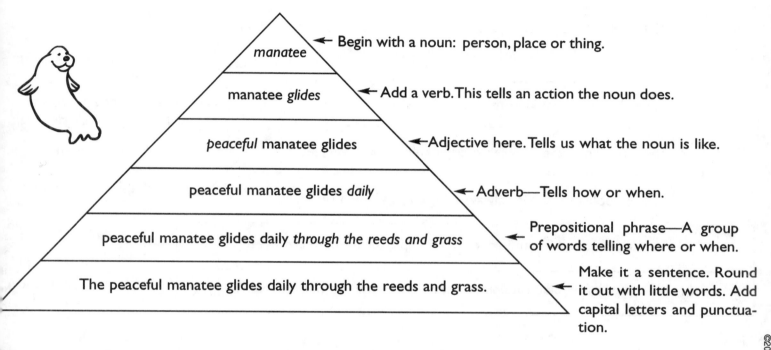

manatee ← Begin with a noun: person, place or thing.

manatee *glides* ← Add a verb. This tells an action the noun does.

peaceful manatee glides ← Adjective here. Tells us what the noun is like.

peaceful manatee glides *daily* ← Adverb—Tells how or when.

peaceful manatee glides daily *through the reeds and grass* ← Prepositional phrase—A group of words telling where or when.

The peaceful manatee glides daily through the reeds and grass. ← Make it a sentence. Round it out with little words. Add capital letters and punctuation.

ow you try one. You need to add a verb (an action for your noun), an adjective (describing the noun), an adverb (telling ow or when), the prepositional phrase (where or when) and finish the sentence.

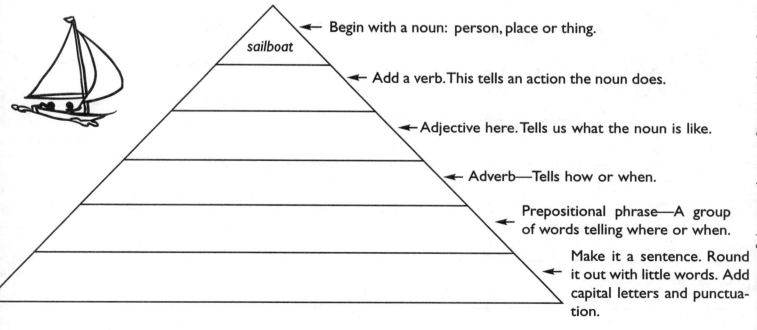

sailboat ← Begin with a noun: person, place or thing.

← Add a verb. This tells an action the noun does.

← Adjective here. Tells us what the noun is like.

← Adverb—Tells how or when.

← Prepositional phrase—A group of words telling where or when.

← Make it a sentence. Round it out with little words. Add capital letters and punctuation.

Slalom Sentences: Pinch Hitter 1

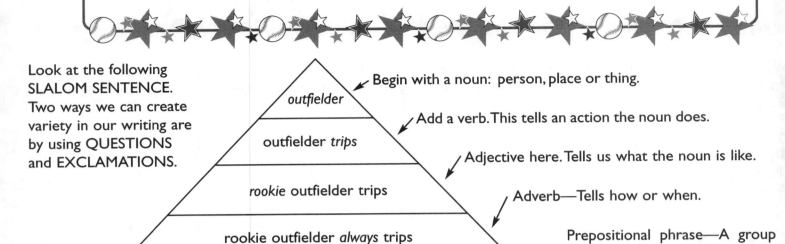

Look at the following SLALOM SENTENCE. Two ways we can create variety in our writing are by using QUESTIONS and EXCLAMATIONS.

outfielder — Begin with a noun: person, place or thing.

outfielder *trips* — Add a verb. This tells an action the noun does.

rookie outfielder trips — Adjective here. Tells us what the noun is like.

rookie outfielder *always* trips — Adverb—Tells how or when.

rookie outfielder always trips *over his own two feet* — Prepositional phrase—A group of words telling where or when.

The rookie outfielder always trips over his own two feet. — Make it a sentence. Round it out with little words. Add capital letters and punctuation.

Why does the rookie outfielder always trip over his own two feet? — Turn the statement into a question.

He blew it! That rookie outfielder always trips over his own two feet! — Turn the statement into an exclamation.

Now you try. Build the SLALOM SENTENCE and then try to make a QUESTION and an EXCLAMATION.

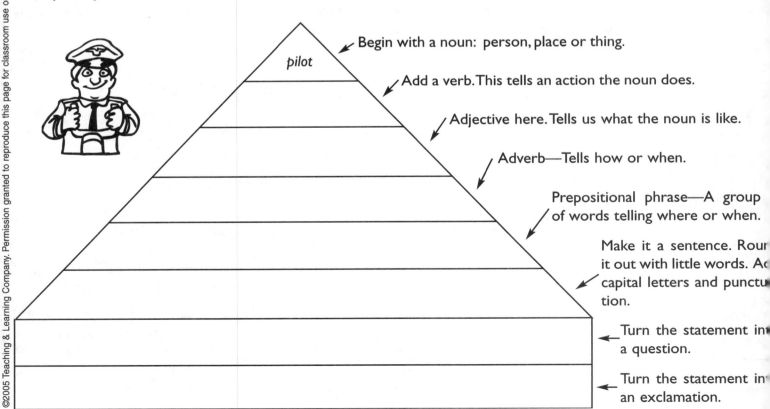

pilot — Begin with a noun: person, place or thing.

Add a verb. This tells an action the noun does.

Adjective here. Tells us what the noun is like.

Adverb—Tells how or when.

Prepositional phrase—A group of words telling where or when.

Make it a sentence. Round it out with little words. Add capital letters and punctuation.

Turn the statement into a question.

Turn the statement into an exclamation.

TLC10471 Copyright © Teaching & Learning Company, Carthage, IL 62321-0

Look at the following SLALOM SENTENCE. Two ways we can create variety in our writing are by using an ADJECTIVE FIRST or a PREPOSITION FIRST.

outfielder → Begin with a noun: person, place or thing.

outfielder *trips* → Add a verb. This tells an action the noun does.

rookie outfielder trips → Adjective here. Tells us what the noun is like.

rookie outfielder *always* trips → Adverb—Tells how or when.

rookie outfielder always trips *over his own two feet* → Prepositional phrase—A group of words telling where or when.

The rookie outfielder always trips over his own two feet. → Make it a sentence. Round it out with little words. Add capital letters and punctuation.

Clumsy, the rookie outfielder always trips over his own two feet. ← Adjective first.

Over his own two feet, the rookie outfielder always trips. ← Preposition first.

Now you try. Build the SLALOM SENTENCE and then try to use an ADJECTIVE FIRST or a PREPOSITION FIRST.

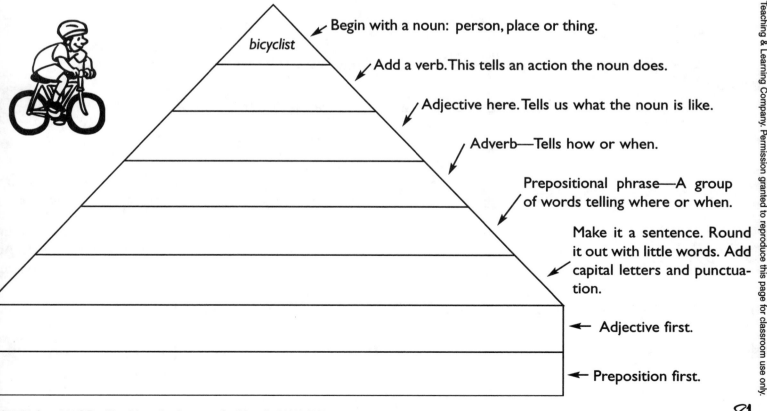

bicyclist → Begin with a noun: person, place or thing.

→ Add a verb. This tells an action the noun does.

→ Adjective here. Tells us what the noun is like.

→ Adverb—Tells how or when.

→ Prepositional phrase—A group of words telling where or when.

→ Make it a sentence. Round it out with little words. Add capital letters and punctuation.

← Adjective first.

← Preposition first.

Slalom Sentences: Pinch Hitter 3

Look at the following SLALOM SENTENCE. Two ways that we can create variety in our writing are by using an APPOSITIVE, almost like a descriptive aside using parentheses, or start with the ADVERB.

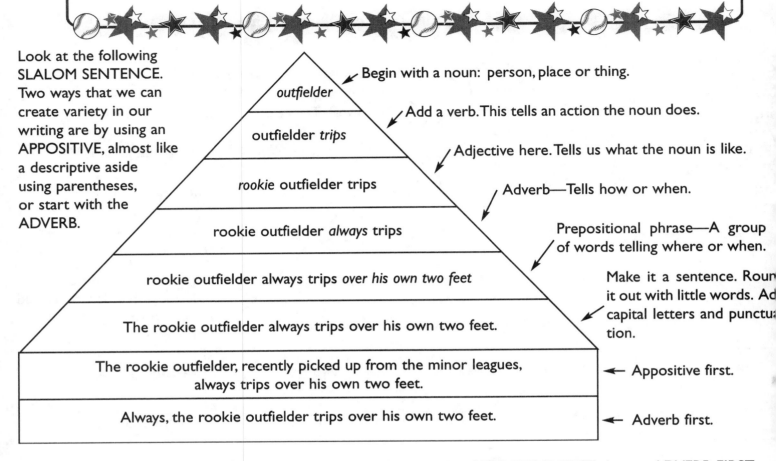

outfielder — Begin with a noun: person, place or thing.

outfielder *trips* — Add a verb. This tells an action the noun does.

rookie outfielder trips — Adjective here. Tells us what the noun is like.

rookie outfielder *always* trips — Adverb—Tells how or when.

rookie outfielder always trips *over his own two feet* — Prepositional phrase—A group of words telling where or when.

The rookie outfielder always trips over his own two feet. — Make it a sentence. Round it out with little words. Add capital letters and punctuation.

The rookie outfielder, recently picked up from the minor leagues, always trips over his own two feet. ← Appositive first.

Always, the rookie outfielder trips over his own two feet. ← Adverb first.

Now you try. Build the SLALOM SENTENCE and then try to use an APPOSITIVE FIRST, then an ADVERB FIRST.

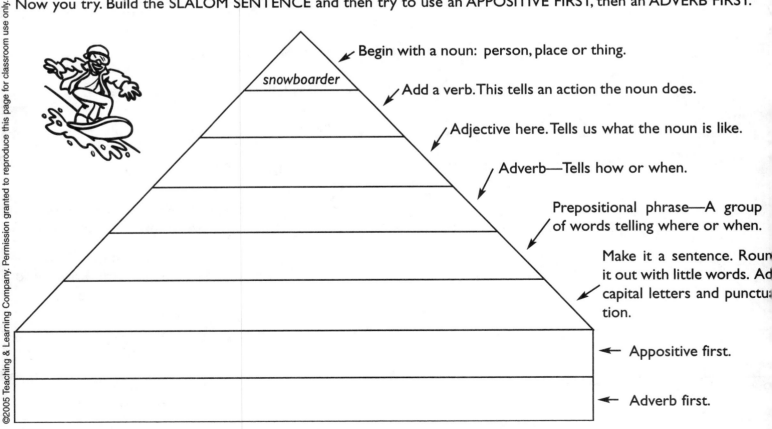

snowboarder — Begin with a noun: person, place or thing.

Add a verb. This tells an action the noun does.

Adjective here. Tells us what the noun is like.

Adverb—Tells how or when.

Prepositional phrase—A group of words telling where or when.

Make it a sentence. Round it out with little words. Add capital letters and punctuation.

← Appositive first.

← Adverb first.

Curve Ball Sentences

Rookie writers don't always think about their sentence structure. Writers who use the same sentence structure are like a pitcher who only knows how to throw one kind of pitch. After a while, the pitcher isn't very interesting to watch and his throws never take the batter by surprise.

The exercise on this page will show you one way to change your sentences. THIS IS VERY IMPORTANT: This is not the way to start all your sentences because if you do then you'll be pitching your writing the same way all over again. This method is like a good curve ball—throw it occasionally.

Read this paragraph.

The girls looked forward to their beach day. They wandered along the shore searching intently for shark's teeth as soon as they got there. They gobbled down a delicious lunch later that day. They body surfed in the refreshing ocean as the sun became an orange streamer in the sky. They left soon after, happy to have spent such a lovely day together.

What's wrong with that paragraph? Even though the description and the word choice were good, the structure was very repetitive. The sentences all sounded the same because they were all constructed with the same pattern.

The subject was placed first, then the predicate and then the details about why, when, how or where came last.

What if we changed the word order in some of those sentences? The paragraph would be more interesting to read! Let's try it.

The girls looked forward to their beach day. As soon as they got there, they wandered along the shore searching intently for shark's teeth. They gobbled down a delicious lunch later that day. When the sun became an orange streamer in the sky, they body-surfed in the refreshing ocean. They left soon after, happy to have spent such a lovely day together.

Do you see how changing one or two sentences can improve your writing?

Here's a sentence written the usual way:

The carpenter dismantled the cabinet with nothing more than a screwdriver.

If we separated the sentence into parts it might look like this:

Subject	Predicate	Phrase that tells how
The carpenter	**dismantled the cabinet**	**with nothing more than a screwdriver**

What if we told how she dismantled that cabinet first?

With nothing more than a screwdriver, the carpenter dismantled the cabinet.

It tells the same information, but in a different way.

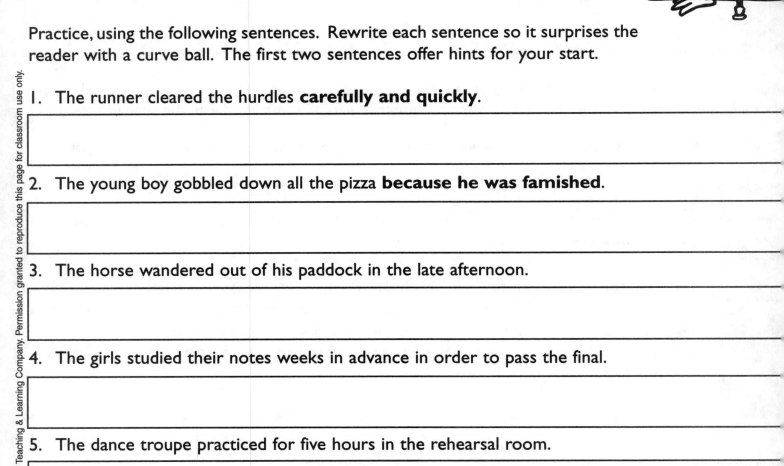

Practice, using the following sentences. Rewrite each sentence so it surprises the reader with a curve ball. The first two sentences offer hints for your start.

1. The runner cleared the hurdles **carefully and quickly**.

_____

2. The young boy gobbled down all the pizza **because he was famished**.

_____

3. The horse wandered out of his paddock in the late afternoon.

_____

4. The girls studied their notes weeks in advance in order to pass the final.

_____

5. The dance troupe practiced for five hours in the rehearsal room.

_____

Leads & Endings

Openings and Conclusions

Coach's Playbook
Leads & Endings

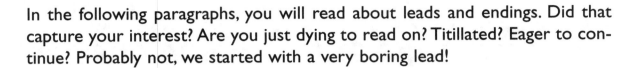

In the following paragraphs, you will read about leads and endings. Did that capture your interest? Are you just dying to read on? Titillated? Eager to continue? Probably not, we started with a very boring lead!

Even if the body of the paper succeeds with details, word choices, description and style, the reader has to be enticed to read beyond the first sentences of the piece. Mastering the skill of the lead can be tough for young writers. This section of the book provides four kinds of leads that can work with all kinds of writing: ACTION LEAD, QUICK PICTURE BLASTS, SETTING THE SCENE and the QUESTION LEAD. Each is presented, explained and modeled. Writers are then invited to try them out.

Maybe the favorite part of a paper for students is the end, because they seem to love putting a huge label after the final paragraph announcing that THE END has been reached. A successful ending restates the main concepts or ties up loose ends, but still leaves the reader with a tasty morsel to chew on. Four endings, THE CHALLENGE, THE PREDICTION, THE PERSONAL CONNECTION and THE INVITATION, are presented for students to experiment with.

Discuss and practice these leads and endings with your students. Feel free to give them additional practice that coordinates with the themes and content of your curriculum.

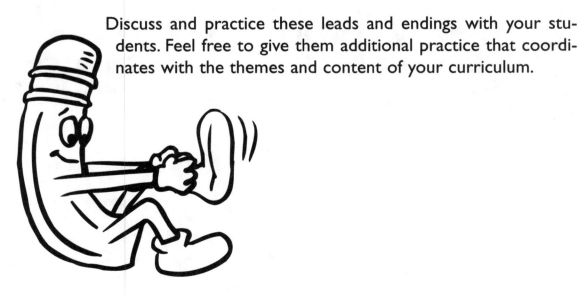

A lead in writing is like hitting a home run on your first at-bat in an important game. A great start usually means a great score. The same is true for writing. A great lead makes the reader want to read more, and isn't that the point? Thinking up a strong lead isn't hard when you've read enough models and you've practiced. When it comes to practice, this is the right place!

LEAD

LEAD 1: ACTION
The action lead starts with action! It's an exciting way to kick off a piece of writing. When we talk about action, that means VERBS—active verbs will be doing the major sweating. Check out the examples below, paying special attention to the verbs in bold print.

ACTION LEADS

A. Crash! The rock **hurled** past the black cat and **shattered** the front window of my neighbor's house. I wanted to scare the yowling cat, and now I found myself on the horns of a dilemma. I **pondered** the problem, and then I **bolted**.

B. Crackle! Boom! The thunder **bounced** off our cabin walls. The windows **rattled** and the front door **shook**. I **searched** everywhere for Buddy, our dog, who was terrified of storms. I **glanced** at the back door. It was wide open.

C. Thwack! The branch **snapped** as I rode by it. I **escaped** its backlash, but my pal Terry hadn't been so lucky. Swinging back in a slow circle, I **pedaled** back to the lump on the ground.

EXAMPLES

NOW YOU TRY

BATTING PRACTICE: For each of these situations, write an action lead.

A. This is a story about a baseball game, where a foul ball hurls straight toward you.

_____

_____

_____

B. This is a paper on bike safety.

_____

_____

_____

Home Run Leads 2

A lead in writing is like hitting a home run on your first at-bat in an important game. A great start usually means a great score. The same is true for writing. A great lead makes the reader want to read more, and isn't that the point? Thinking up a strong lead isn't hard when you've read enough models and you've practiced. When it comes to practice, this is the right place!

LEAD

LEAD 2: QUICK PICTURE BLAST

Quick Picture Blast is about using quick and interesting images to begin your story. This is an adjective/noun partnership that can startle your readers and make them want to read further. Look at the examples below of these adjective/noun partnerships.

EXAMPLES

QUICK PICTURE BLAST LEADS

A. **Runny noses! Scraped knees! So many questions!** Doing a baby-sitting favor for my aunt proved to be hazardous to my health!

B. **Breathtaking vistas!   Brilliant sunsets!   Majestic canyons!**   Everyone should visit the Southwest on their next vacation.

C. **Soaring leaps! Dizzying turns! Nimble choreography!** Going to the ballet with my grandfather opened my eyes to the marvels of this great art.

NOW YOU TRY

BATTING PRACTICE: For each of these situations, write a quick picture blast lead.

A.   This is a story about being caught in a severe thunderstorm.

_____

_____

_____

B.   This is a paper on the dangers of playing with fire.

_____

_____

_____

 TLC10471 Copyright © Teaching & Learning Company, Carthage, IL 62321-001

Home Run Leads 3

A lead in writing is like hitting a home run on your first at-bat in an important game. A great start usually means a great score. The same is true for writing. A great lead makes the reader want to read more, and isn't that the point? Thinking up a strong lead isn't hard when you've read enough models and you've practiced. When it comes to practice, this is the right place!

 **LEAD**

LEAD 3: SETTING THE SCENE
Setting the scene is all about using sensory details to establish a sense of place. Using words that tell about sight, smell, touch, hearing and taste will help you with this kind of lead. Finish your lead with the topic statement.

SETTING THE SCENE LEADS

A. My father's favorite golf shoes were chewed beyond recognition. Paper shreds from the phone book covered the living room floor. Dirt from an overturned plant littered one corner of the kitchen. I quickly realized that it's important to spend time training a dog.

B. The curtains reeked of old tobacco. On tables everywhere, the ashtrays overflowed. In his favorite chair, my uncle hacked and coughed every 10 minutes. Why does anyone ever start smoking?

C. The palm trees swayed with the afternoon breeze. Ocean mist tickled my nose with hints of salt. The warm sand oozed between my toes. Beach vacations are, without question, my favorite.

EXAMPLES

BATTING PRACTICE: For each of these situations, write a setting the scene lead.

A. This is a story about going camping in the mountains.

_____

_____

B. This is a paper on your favorite holiday.

_____

_____

_____

NOW YOU TRY

TLC10471 Copyright © Teaching & Learning Company, Carthage, IL 62321-0010

Home Run Leads 4

A lead in writing is like hitting a home run on your first at-bat in an important game. A great start usually means [a] great score. The same is true for writing. A great lead makes the reader want to read more, and isn't that the point? Thinking up a strong lead isn't hard when you've read enough models and you've practiced. When it comes to practice, this is the right place!

LEAD

LEAD 4: QUESTION
Question leads need the writer to think of unique and interesting questions to tease their reader. IF IT'S A QUESTION THE READER CAN ANSWER, THEN YOU ARE OUT OF THE GAME! A strong and original question captures a reader's interest and makes him or her want to read further. It takes some thinking, but just the right question can have your writing flying out of the ballpark!

QUESTION LEADS

A. When is lunch time like an action movie? If your school is being remodeled, there are heroic adjustments to be made in your day.

B. What do you get when you mix a grouchy neighbor, a thunderstorm and two dozen brownies? Sometimes terrible weather can bring people together.

EXAMPLES

C. What famous American never had formal schooling but was responsible for establishing a lending library, designing bifocals and was the best-known writer of his time? These truthful descriptors are part of the fascinating life of Benjamin Franklin.

NOW YOU TRY

BATTING PRACTICE: For each of these situations, write a question lead.

A. This is a story about going to visit your least favorite relative.

_____

_____

_____

B. This is a paper on the best way to make a good impression.

_____

_____

_____

90

you start off strong, it doesn't always mean that you'll win the game. A true champion completes every inning at full ower. The same is true for writing. A successful ending will leave your reader satisfied and enriched.

ENDING

ENDING 1: CHALLENGE
The challenge ending gives readers something to think about even after they finish reading your paper. It can be in the form of a question, but doesn't have to be. Challenge endings ask your readers to take action or to consider another possibility.

CHALLENGE ENDINGS
A. Needless to say, the day was a mess. Do you think you would have the patience to put up with construction chaos in your school?

B. In my neighborhood, we're thankful that the storm came. Don't wait for a natural disaster to bond with the people you see every day.

C. Think about all the advantages you have: education, electricity and insurance. Will you be able to achieve half as much as Ben Franklin, who started with so little?

EXAMPLES

NOW YOU TRY

SLIDING DRILL: For each of these situations, create a challenge ending.

A. This is a story about going to the dentist.

_____

_____

B. This is a paper on the best way to study for a test.

_____

_____

_____

If you start off strong, it doesn't always mean that you'll win the game. A true champion completes every inning at fu[l] power. The same is true for writing. A successful ending will leave your reader satisfied and enriched.

ENDING

ENDING 2: PREDICTION
A prediction ending is the writer's guess as to what may happen in the future. It encourages readers to think about the writing and make their own predictions as well.

EXAMPLES

PREDICTION ENDINGS

A. Training a dog properly can make the difference between remodeling and home sweet home. I bet my father will make sure he sends our next dog to obedience school.

B. Smoking ruined my uncle's life. I think every one of his children will always avoid smoking.

C. Beach living is mesmerizing. I'm sure I'll be back next year!

NOW YOU TRY

SLIDING DRILL: For each of these situations, create a prediction ending.

A. This is a story about going camping in the mountains.

_____

_____

_____

B. This is a paper on your favorite class in school.

_____

_____

_____

_____

you start off strong, it doesn't always mean that you'll win the game. A true champion completes every inning at full power. The same is true for writing. A successful ending will leave your reader satisfied and enriched.

ENDING

ENDING 3: PERSONAL CONNECTION
A personal connection ending tells how the writer feels about his or her topic overall. It taps the writer's emotions or opinions and expresses a connection or relationship to the topic.

PERSONAL CONNECTION ENDING

A. When the day was done, I survived the ordeal and performed a great favor for my aunt. I'm quite sure that I won't be making baby-sitting my career choice.

B. My album is filled with dozens of pictures of the Grand Canyon. I'll never forget that very special trip with my family.

C. The memory of that performance still leaves me breathless. I wish everyone could experience the grace and beauty of a live ballet performance.

EXAMPLES

NOW YOU TRY

SLIDING DRILL: For each of these situations, create a personal connection ending.

A. This is a story about being caught in a severe thunderstorm.

_____

_____

_____

B. This is a paper on the dangers of playing with fire.

_____

_____

_____

©2005 Teaching & Learning Company. Permission granted to reproduce this page for classroom use only.

If you start off strong, it doesn't always mean that you'll win the game. A true champion completes every inning at full power. The same is true for writing. A successful ending will leave your reader satisfied and enriched.

ENDING

ENDING 4: INVITATION
An invitation ending encourages the reader to join the writer in his or her conclusion. It's an acknowledgment that you've shared a unique journey.

EXAMPLES

INVITATION ENDING

A. In the end, I learned that honesty was the best policy. If we own up to our actions and take what's coming to us, we'll feel better in the end, don't you think?

B. With the help of our neighbors, this particular story had a happy ending. Working together we can all protect the animals that love us.

C. The day ended with a two-hour wait in the emergency room and 24 stitches to Terry's forehead. Keeping a level head and staying calm is the best medicine when a friend is hurt.

NOW YOU TRY

SLIDING DRILL: For each of these situations, create an invitation ending.

A. This is a story about a baseball game where a foul ball hurls straight toward you.

_____

_____

B. This is a paper on bike safety.

_____

_____

_____

Play Ball!

Drafts for Practicing and Evaluation

Coach's Playbook
Play Ball!

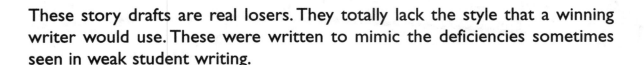

These story drafts are real losers. They totally lack the style that a winning writer would use. These were written to mimic the deficiencies sometimes seen in weak student writing.

You may choose to use these drafts to practice one or two of the skill sets presented in the first section of the book, or use them for a cumulative application of all eight parts. Have students diagnose the weaknesses and recommend strategies to build some muscle tone in this wimpy writing.

These anonymous weak writing samples can be used in the classroom without concern for the ego bruises that sometimes occur when using actual student samples.

TLC10471 Copyright © Teaching & Learning Company, Carthage, IL 62321-001

One day my grandma came to visit. My grandma is cool and does cool things. I like when she visits.

My friend came over and wanted me to play. I told him my grandma was here. I was going to do stuff with her. He got mad and said I was weird. I told him my grandma was cool.

He left and I felt bad. I told my grandma. She said she had an idea. She told me the idea. I said okay.

I called my friend and told him we were going someplace cool. I said my grandma was taking me. He could come along. He said okay. He came with us.

We got there. We had fun with the three of us. My friend liked being with my grandma. He didn't think I was weird anymore.

Second Inning

One day I went to school. When I got there, a new student was in our class. She seemed okay. She sat down next to me.

At lunch she ate by herself. No one talked to her. I thought maybe I should talk to her but I thought she might be weird.

At recess, she sat by a tree by herself. She looked really sad. I walked over and started to talk to her. She was really funny. She knew a lot of jokes. We started laughing.

The other kids heard us laugh. They came over. She told more jokes. The other kids started to laugh, too. I didn't think she was weird anymore. Now she is my best friend.

Third Inning

This is about a time I went to a party. It was so fun.

My friend was having a birthday party. She called me up to invite me and I said yes. I couldn't wait to go. So I went in the house and there was a big party with all these decorations in all these colors and stuff on the walls and on the windows.

We played some games. We played inside with a CD player and some music. Someone didn't win and cried. That person kicked the table and the cake fell off. It hit the ground. It was a mess.

My friend cried when she saw her cake on the floor. She felt awful. She looked awful. Her mom tried to make her feel better. I had an idea. I called my mother. We live close to a bakery. My mother came back with a cake for my friend. My friend felt better. She was happy.

That was a time I helped. I was glad.

Fourth Inning

One time I was home on a Saturday. It was raining a little, then a lot. There was thunder and lightning, and then the lights went out. Everything went off. We had no electricity.

I didn't know what to do. I was bored. I looked in my room and couldn't find anything to do. It was boring. I sat in the closet I was so bored. Something was in the corner. It was a game.

Maybe my brother would want to play. I asked him. He was bored, too, and said okay. We played. The game was hard to win but it was fun. We played a long time.

The lights came back on. The game was so fun. We kept on. Now we play that game all the time even when there's no storm.

Fifth Inning

One morning I woke up. I ate then I went to the park. At the park I saw my friend, and we decided to have ice cream. We paid the man. Then we went to play.

We went to play on the swings. We went high. My friend went high then fell. My friend was crying. Her ankle got real big.

I knew I had to help. No one was around. Her ankle was getting really big. She looked really hurt. I remembered the ice cream man. I went to get ice.

I got ice and put it on my friend's ankle. My friend said it felt better with the ice. My friend got up. I helped her walk home. Then I went home.

Sixth Inning

One day I went to the park. No one was there, so I went on the swings by myself. I had fun.

Then I walked around. I found a puppy under a bench. He was cute. I always wanted a puppy. He licked my face. I decided to bring him home.

On the way home, I saw some signs. They said LOST PUPPY. The signs had the picture of the puppy and a sad little girl. It was her puppy.

But I wanted to keep the puppy. It was cute. If I kept it, no one would know about it being lost. I could get rid of all the signs. Then I looked at the sad girl on the sign. I felt bad. I decided to take the puppy to her.

I went to the house. I brought the puppy. She was very happy and so was the puppy. I felt better.

Seventh Inning

Have you ever found something? I have. This is the story.

First I got up and I went outside. I was walking and I found a bag. It wasn't heavy. I picked it up and looked inside. There were jewels inside. I was so happy.

Next, I called my friend and told her what happened. She said I was so lucky. She wanted to know what I was going to do. I didn't know. She said I should keep the jewels because then I could sell them. I still didn't know what to do.

I wanted to ask my mom but I knew she would tell me to turn it in. I knew my mom needed a new car and these would help her. I decided to think and think. I watched some television. I saw something on the news. Some stuff had been stolen from a store. I bet it was the jewels.

Next I called them. I told them I found some jewels. They said to come down and show them. I said I would. So I did and I got a reward and my mom put it away to help buy a new car. Honesty pays sometimes.

Eighth Inning

This is how my birthday party was so fun.

First of all, we had some games. We played water balloon tag. Then we played Tug of War. Then we played Hit the Piñata. It was fun.

Next, we ate lots of good stuff. There was a big cake shaped like my favorite toy. It was delicious. Everyone ate a bunch of it.

Finally, we had live entertainment. We hired some guy to do some magic. He did some tricks and told some jokes. Everyone laughed and was amazed at all the things he did.

Then it was over and everyone went home.

TLC10471 Copyright © Teaching & Learning Company, Carthage, IL 62321-0

Ninth Inning

This is why writing is important.

First of all, it's important in school. In school you write a lot. You write for many subjects. It is easy.

In addition, writing is helpful. If someone is sick, I can write them a letter. If someone is sad, I can write them a note. If someone is happy, I can write them and tell them I am happy, too.

Last, writing can be fun. You can make up things. You can make up stories. You can make up poems. You can make up comic strips.

I like to write.

Play Ball!

Now you're ready for the big leagues. Scout out the samples from each of the innings and note it on this scorecard. Are they losing? Make a game plan to turn that loser into a winner!

Play	Winner?	Loser?	You're the Coach: Game plan to fix it
Elaboration—Details	_____	_____	_____ _____ _____
Vocabulary Muscle— Choosing the Right Words	_____	_____	_____ _____ _____
Descriptivitis—Using Moderation in Description	_____	_____	_____ _____ _____
Dead Verbs— Burying Bad Verb Habits	_____	_____	_____ _____ _____
Show, Don't Tell— Using Action and Specifics	_____	_____	_____ _____ _____
Fast Forward & Slow Motion— Pacing the Action	_____	_____	_____ _____ _____
Varying the Game Plan— Sentence Variety	_____	_____	_____ _____ _____
Leads & Endings— Openings and Conclusions	_____	_____	_____ _____ _____

TLC10471 Copyright © Teaching & Learning Company, Carthage, IL 62321-0

Play Ball!

Now you're ready for the big leagues. Scout out the samples from each of the innings and note it on this scorecard. Are they losing? Make a game plan to turn that loser into a winner!

Play	Winner?	Loser?	You're the Coach: Game plan to fix it
Elaboration—Details	_____	_____	_____ _____ _____
Vocabulary Muscle—Choosing the Right Words	_____	_____	_____ _____ _____
Descriptivitis—Using Moderation in Description	_____	_____	_____ _____ _____
Dead Verbs—Burying Bad Verb Habits	_____	_____	_____ _____ _____
Show, Don't Tell—Using Action and Specifics	_____	_____	_____ _____ _____
Fast Forward & Slow Motion—Pacing the Action	_____	_____	_____ _____ _____
Varying the Game Plan—Sentence Variety	_____	_____	_____ _____ _____
Leads & Endings—Openings and Conclusions	_____	_____	_____ _____ _____

Play Ball!

Now you're ready for the big leagues. Scout out the samples from each of the innings and note it on this scorecard. Are they losing? Make a game plan to turn that loser into a winner!

Play	Winner?	Loser?	You're the Coach: Game plan to fix it
Elaboration—Details	_____	_____	_____ _____ _____
Vocabulary Muscle— Choosing the Right Words	_____	_____	_____ _____
Descriptivitis—Using Moderation in Description	_____	_____	_____ _____
Dead Verbs— Burying Bad Verb Habits	_____	_____	_____ _____
Show, Don't Tell— Using Action and Specifics	_____	_____	_____ _____
Fast Forward & Slow Motion— Pacing the Action	_____	_____	_____ _____
Varying the Game Plan— Sentence Variety	_____	_____	_____ _____
Leads & Endings— Openings and Conclusions	_____	_____	_____ _____

Play Ball!

Now you're ready for the big leagues. Scout out the samples from each of the innings and note it on this scorecard. Are they losing? Make a game plan to turn that loser into a winner!

Play	Winner?	Loser?	You're the Coach: Game plan to fix it
Elaboration—Details	_____	_____	_____ _____ _____
Vocabulary Muscle—Choosing the Right Words	_____	_____	_____ _____ _____
Descriptivitis—Using Moderation in Description	_____	_____	_____ _____ _____
Dead Verbs—Burying Bad Verb Habits	_____	_____	_____ _____ _____
Show, Don't Tell—Using Action and Specifics	_____	_____	_____ _____ _____
Fast Forward & Slow Motion—Pacing the Action	_____	_____	_____ _____ _____
Varying the Game Plan—Sentence Variety	_____	_____	_____ _____ _____
Leads & Endings—Openings and Conclusions	_____	_____	_____ _____ _____

Play Ball!

Now you're ready for the big leagues. Scout out the samples from each of the innings and note it on this scorecard. Are they losing? Make a game plan to turn that loser into a winner!

Play	Winner?	Loser?	You're the Coach: Game plan to fix it
Elaboration—Details	_____	_____	_____ _____ _____
Vocabulary Muscle— Choosing the Right Words	_____	_____	_____ _____ _____
Descriptivitis—Using Moderation in Description	_____	_____	_____ _____ _____
Dead Verbs— Burying Bad Verb Habits	_____	_____	_____ _____ _____
Show, Don't Tell— Using Action and Specifics	_____	_____	_____ _____ _____
Fast Forward & Slow Motion— Pacing the Action	_____	_____	_____ _____ _____
Varying the Game Plan— Sentence Variety	_____	_____	_____ _____ _____
Leads & Endings— Openings and Conclusions	_____	_____	_____ _____ _____

Play Ball!

Now you're ready for the big leagues. Scout out the samples from each of the innings and note it on this scorecard. Are they losing? Make a game plan to turn that loser into a winner!

Play	Winner?	Loser?	You're the Coach: Game plan to fix it
Elaboration—Details	_____	_____	_____ _____ _____
Vocabulary Muscle— Choosing the Right Words	_____	_____	_____ _____ _____
Descriptivitis—Using Moderation in Description	_____	_____	_____ _____ _____
Dead Verbs— Burying Bad Verb Habits	_____	_____	_____ _____ _____
Show, Don't Tell— Using Action and Specifics	_____	_____	_____ _____ _____
Fast Forward & Slow Motion— Pacing the Action	_____	_____	_____ _____ _____
Varying the Game Plan— Sentence Variety	_____	_____	_____ _____ _____
Leads & Endings— Openings and Conclusions	_____	_____	_____ _____ _____

Play Ball!

Now you're ready for the big leagues. Scout out the samples from each of the innings and note it on this scorecard. Are they losing? Make a game plan to turn that loser into a winner!

Play	Winner?	Loser?	You're the Coach: Game plan to fix it
Elaboration—Details	_____	_____	_____ _____ _____
Vocabulary Muscle— Choosing the Right Words	_____	_____	_____ _____ _____
Descriptivitis—Using Moderation in Description	_____	_____	_____ _____ _____
Dead Verbs— Burying Bad Verb Habits	_____	_____	_____ _____ _____
Show, Don't Tell— Using Action and Specifics	_____	_____	_____ _____ _____
Fast Forward & Slow Motion— Pacing the Action	_____	_____	_____ _____ _____
Varying the Game Plan— Sentence Variety	_____	_____	_____ _____ _____
Leads & Endings— Openings and Conclusions	_____	_____	_____ _____ _____